DESIGNED FOR
LIVING

EDITED BY CORNELIUS O'DONNELL

AVERY PUBLISHING GROUP INC.
Garden City Park, New York

Library of Congress Cataloging-in-Publication Data
Designed for living Corning cookbook : quick, healthy, and delicious
recipes / Cornelius O'Donnell, editor.
  p.   cm.
  Includes index.
  ISBN 0-89529-551-2 : $24.95
  1. Quick and easy cookery. 2. Menus. I. O'Donnell, Cornelius.
TX833.5.D47   1992
641.5—dc20   92-21725
                                                           CIP

All products featured in Designed for Living Corning Cookbook are
listed in the photo credits sections, pages 185–187.

CONTENTS

COOKING WELL

"We may live without friends; we may live without books;
But civilized man can not live without cooks . . .
He may live without love—what is passion but pining?
But where is the man who can live without dining?"

So wrote Edward, Earl of Lytton, more than a century ago. The same holds true of men and women today. Dining well is considered by many to be one of life's primary pleasures. But cooking well can provide even more enjoyment, satisfaction, and a far greater sense of accomplishment.

Whether it's simple family fare or a gourmet feast, preparing a delicious, attractive meal can be a truly rewarding experience—especially for the person who regards cooking as an outlet for creative juices rather than a necessary evil or time-consuming chore. This book was created by Corning with that in mind. It is designed to make the contemporary chef's sojourn in the kitchen easy, fast, and as much fun as possible.

We offer a variety of recipes with an international flavor, bold new American dishes, and updated versions of classic favorites. You'll find basic information about cooking techniques, health and nutrition, menu suggestions, hints on food preparation, and time-saving tips.

Recipes may be accompanied by the following symbols:

Nonfat or low-fat— ●   Low calorie— ■   Vegetarian entree— ▼

Many of the recipes include suggestions for adaptations or alternate ingredients that will further lower the fat and/or cholesterol content. Using low-fat or nonfat substitutes for dairy products, mayonnaise, broths etc., will significantly lower the overall fat, cholesterol, and calorie content of each recipe.

PLAN AHEAD

Cooking a simple meal or a gourmet feast can be easy and fun for the chef—with just a little advance planning. The keys to success are organization and preparation.

First and foremost, plan your meal—the number of courses, types of food, and recipes. In choosing the menu, keep in mind your cooking skills and the time required to prepare the ingredients and cook.

To expand your cooking repertoire, try out new recipes and techniques on family and very close friends first rather than on guests. That alone will eliminate a lot of stress and anxiety. When entertaining, cook and serve dishes that you already know how to make.

GETTING STARTED

You've shopped, the ingredients are on hand, and you're ready to begin. Here are two absolute rules to follow before you start cooking that will make your time in the kitchen more fun and rewarding:

1. **Always read the recipe through.**
2. **Assemble all the ingredients, cleaned, prepared, and measured.**

Here's a tip to help avoid mistakes and omissions: For each recipe, clean, prepare, and measure the ingredients and place them on a tray. In the case of ingredients that must be kept refrigerated, write the name of each ingredient on a separate card and put the cards on the tray. This may seem simplistic, but try it—you won't leave anything out! Also, keep in mind that, to save time, many items can be cleaned, prepared, and measured while other ingredients are cooking.

Ratatouille, see p. 108.

1

OUTFITTING THE KITCHEN FOR GOOD COOKING

There are no hard-and-fast rules regarding kitchen equipment: it's *your* kitchen, and you and your family's needs and interests are unique. It is true, however, that certain kitchen equipment is essential to good cooking whether you cook for one, two, or more. The following pages offer lists of the basic utensils and appliances needed to produce meals for four to six people.

Buy the best-quality tools that you can afford—particularly when it comes to pots, pans, and knives, which get hard use in any kitchen. Good-quality tools last longer and give more consistent results in the long run. A few high-quality pieces of cookware are better than a kitchenful of things that won't last and may not be right for you.

Before investing (or reinvesting) in any kitchen equipment, take stock of your situation and special needs. How big is your family? Do you entertain a lot? How large is your kitchen and how much storage space is available? Are you and your family always on the go? Your answers will be key to estimating your equipment needs.

You probably already have a variety of pans and knives on your kitchen shelves. Start by taking inventory. Give the pans you never use to someone else who will. If you avoid using some pans because of the way they perform, get rid of them. If your knives are so dull that they can barely slice butter, maybe it's time for new ones . . . the best you can afford.

When it comes to pots and pans, look for sturdy, durable ones that won't dent or warp with heat. Tight-fitting lids and heat-proof handles are also important. Stainless-steel cookware with either copper or aluminum bottoms for even heating are very popular. The advent of the microwave oven makes versatile, multipurpose pans increasingly important in today's kitchen. Glass-ceramic cookware that goes from range top to oven to microwave to broiler is especially useful when storage space is at a premium. Nesting is another space-saving virtue of many of these new products.

Besides easy cleanup, there's another reason to consider nonstick cookware. If your diet demands low-fat cooking, nonstick pans and skillets let you cook with little or no fat. Microwave-compatible nonstick cookware is twice as useful. Another essential for low-fat cooking is a vegetable steamer. A separate pan or a steamer insert that fits into a regular pan is another space saver.

Attractive cookware that goes from the stove or oven to the table saves space and reduces cleanup—a boon to busy cooks. Such double-duty cookware is very cost-effective because you can get by with one pan or casserole instead of one for cooking and another for serving.

To save more space, look for measuring cups (for both liquid and dry ingredients) and mixing bowls that nest. Mixing bowls that can also be used in the oven save even more storage space.

Knives are another kitchen essential in terms of which top quality is very important. Choose them carefully for weight and balance; you'll have your knives for a lifetime if you care for them properly. Blades made of carbon steel hold their sharpness best, but they also stain and rust unless promptly washed and dried after use; stainless steel is easier to care for but dulls more quickly.

Dull knives are not only harder to work with, they are also more dangerous. Because you have to exert greater pressure when you use a dull knife, the potential of a severe cut is greater if the knife should slip—as it might while deboning, for example. Always keep knives as sharp a possible. That means regular sharpening, either with an electric knife sharpener or a 10-inch sharpening steel. If you buy a sharpening steel, ask the salesperson to demonstrate how to use it correctly.

The number of kitchen gadgets is endless. As your cooking skills develop, you will find them increasingly fascinating. Only a few are truly necessary, however. The others are extras or frills that should be carefully chosen to keep your kitchen miscellany drawer from overflowing. Under the heading Essential Others (see p.3) we list some time-tested "reliables" that you will use frequently.

A comment on spoons, bowls, and cutting boards made of wood: Always clean them well both before and after use. Unlike glass or plastic, wood is porous and can absorb and harbor harmful bacteria. Always scrub wooden cutting boards thoroughly with a mixture of chlorine bleach and hot water after using. Better yet, use glass, plastic or acrylic ones.

Basic Pots and Pans

3 covered saucepans, 1-, 2-, and 3-quart sizes
2 covered skillets/sauté pans, 8- and 10-inch
8-quart covered stockpot
4½-quart covered Dutch oven
2-quart covered double boiler
Steamer
Shallow roasting pan (15 × 10 × 2 inches)
Deep roasting pan with rack (16 × 11½ × 5 inches)
3 *microwaveable* covered round casseroles, in various sizes

Upgrade

12-inch covered *sautôir*
6-quart covered stockpot
6-quart covered Dutch oven

Basic Knives

2 3½-inch-blade paring knives
2 chef's knives, 8- or 9-inch blade
Serrated bread knife
Carving knife and fork
Knife sharpener (10-inch steel or electric sharpener)

Upgrade

5-inch boning knife

Basic Ovenware

9-inch pie plate
8-inch square cake dish
8- or 9-inch round cake dishes
3-quart rectangular baking dish (13 × 9 × 2 inches)
2- or 2½-quart oval casserole
2 covered casseroles, 1½- and 2½-quart
1½-quart loaf pan (8½ × 4½ × 2½ inches)
4 6-ounce custard cups
2 muffin pans
2 cookie sheets (10 × 12½-inch minimum)
9-inch springform pan

Upgrade

2-quart rectangular baking dish
3-quart covered round casserole
5-quart covered oval casserole/roaster
4-quart open roaster
1½-quart loaf pan (additional)
2-quart soufflé dish
4 6-ounce custard cups (additional)

Basic Small Appliances

Blender
Food processor
Microwave oven
Toaster oven
Electric hand mixer

Upgrade

1 griddle
Standing mixer, 5-quart capacity
Waffle iron

Basic Utensils

Long-handled plastic or wooden cooking spoons, one slotted
Whisks, various sizes
Spatulas, metal and rubber
Soup ladle
Kitchen tongs
Kitchen scissors
Meat pounder (the kind shaped like a large thumbtack)
Mixing bowls, 1- or 1½-, 2½-, and 4-quart
Measuring cups:
    Liquid: 1-, 2-, 4-, and 8-cup
    Dry: ¼-, ⅓-, ½-, ⅔-, and 1-cup
Measuring spoon set
Flour sifter   Citrus zester
Rolling pin   4-sided grater
Pastry blender   Bulb baster
Pastry brush   Bottle/can opener
Wire rack   Corkscrew
Vegetable peeler

Essential Others

Teakettle
Coffeepot
Pepper mill
Food mill or grinder
Colander
Cutting board
Storage containers with tight-fitting lids
Kitchen timer
Oven thermometer
Instant-read meat thermometer

Upgrade

Poultry shears
Additional pepper mills
Yogurt funnel
Salad spinner

1) Measuring cups

2) Mixing bowls

3) Storage containers

4) Colander

5) Dutch oven

6) Stockpot

7) Saucepan

8) Double boiler

9) Saucepan with steamer inset

10) Nonstick skillet

11) Sauté pan

12) Sautôir

13) Au gratin dish

14) Cookie sheet

15) Muffin pan

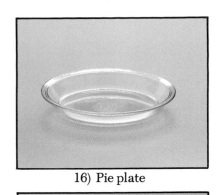
16) Pie plate

17) Cake dish

18) Quiche dish

19) Loaf pan

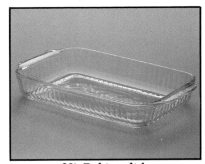
20) Baking dish

21) Roasting pan

22) Lasagna pan

23) Casserole

24) Custard cups

25) Souffle dishes

Each RECIPE in this book includes an equipment list which specifies the optimal size and type of cookware. With the exception of most recipes for baked goods, trade up to a *larger* size if you don't have the right one at hand.

Keep in mind that Dutch ovens can be used on the stovetop and in the oven. You may substitute a saucepan or casserole for a Dutch oven, depending on the cooking method.

If a non-microwave recipe calls for a *covered* baking dish, skillet, sauté pan, casserole, or Dutch oven and all you have is one without a lid, use aluminum foil.

When a glass or ceramic vessel is specified, you really must use one. When some metals come in contact with certain acidic foods, an adverse chemical reaction may result.

Because most cooking involves a fair amount of cutting, it's wise to do all cutting before you actually start cooking. A food processor can make chopping large quantities quick and easy. For small-scale cooking, a good chef's knife and *practice, practice, practice* make this chore fun . . . to say nothing of its being a great outlet for pent-up aggressions!

Here is a quick primer on various cutting techniques done by hand.

Chopping/Mincing: When a recipe calls for "chopped" ingredients, a medium chop is usually meant. With an onion, for example, the pieces should be about half the size of the nail on your little finger. "Finely chopped" or "minced" refer to one-quarter the size of that fingernail, or smaller. Sometimes the origin of the recipe can be a clue to the size of the pieces to be cut. For a rustic country dish, for example, ingredients will usually be roughly chopped; whereas haute cuisine generally calls for more finely chopped food. To chop or mince by hand, slice food such as onions or apples in half lengthwise, place halves cut-side down on a board, and make cuts ¼ inch or less apart, horizontally first, then vertically in two directions (east-west and north-south). Then slice straight down.

To chop or mince leafy foods like parsley, bunch leaves together and cut straight across several times. Then, holding the point of the knife against the cutting board, move the knife up and down over the parsley in a rocking motion. Repeat until finely chopped.

Cubing/Dicing: A recipe will usually specify the cube size needed. If it doesn't, cut ingredients into "bite-sized" square bits; dicing refers to smaller cubes, less than a half inch across. Again, if a recipe is not specific, picture the finished dish in your mind and cut accordingly. Generally, peel food before cutting into cubes. Large squashes and the like, however, are easier to peel after they've been cut into small chunks. For even cooking, especially with microwave recipes, make all pieces approximately the same size. To cube by hand, slice the food, stack, then cut in even-sized strips. Holding several strips together, cut them crosswise into cubes.

Julienning: This technique refers to cutting foods into long, thin "matchstick"-sized pieces—either for quick cooking, as in stir-frying, or for salads or garnish. Again, pieces should be uniform in size. Food processors with julienning disks in various sizes can speed the preparation of large quantities of vegetables. For smaller quantities, it's just as easy to julienne by hand. Thinly slice food, stack, and cut into very thin sticks.

Shredding and Grating: This can be done with either a food processor or a four-sided, stainless-steel hand grater. Using short, quick strokes, rub food over the fine holes of a grater for finely grated food or over the larger holes to shred into thin slivers.

Peeling: Recipes usually say if a vegetable is to be peeled or not. Today's trend is to leave the peel on whenever possible, because it contains many valuable nutrients. Carrots, unless they are extremely old, can simply be scrubbed well and left unpeeled—especially for soups or stews or roasting. Potatoes, too, retain more flavor when they are scrubbed and cooked in their "jackets." To peel or not to peel is a personal choice, of course, but some people even mash potatoes skin and all. "Waxed" vegetables— cucumbers or squash, for example—should always be peeled before eating or cooking.

Zesting: It is amazing how much flavor can be added to so many foods with the addition of the zest (colored outer peel) of citrus fruits. Smart cooks sometimes use it in place of salt. You can use either the fine side of a grater or a handy tool called a **zester**. It has tiny, sharp holes and should be of good quality because zesting puts heavy pressure on the cutting end. Be careful to remove only the top, colored edge of the rind, avoiding the bitter white pithy part. Use short strokes or cut longer pieces of zest with a knife before adding to a dish. Try adding the zest from a lime, lemon, or grapefruit to broiled fish or fruit salad—or even a pasta in cream sauce.

USING THE FOOD PROCESSOR

Food processors are kitchen wonders that chop, dice, grind, mince, shred, slice, and puree—all in a flash. When cooking in quantity, they are very efficient indeed. A little planning can make them even more efficient. Think about how you will use the processor as you put your meal together. If you plan each step, you won't spend valuable time needlessly washing the bowl and blade each time you use the machine. For instance, grate hard cheese or make your bread crumbs (these shake easily out of the container), then chop celery, then puree vegetables. You can do all three—or four—without washing in between.

Helpful Hints

● Garlic or shallots will chop more uniformly if you add them through the food tube with the motor running.
● Processors are particularly good at making pie or tart dough. Use a light touch on the pulse button and don't overmix or the dough will become tough.
● To puree soups, drain off most (*not all!*) of the liquid before adding to the processor so the solids will puree evenly; then add the remaining liquid and finish pureeing the soup. To puree soups in a blender, add equal amounts of solids and liquids; run at the Blend speed for a few seconds at a time. Stir as necessary in between to redistribute ingredients.
● If a recipe calls for several chopped items to be combined (such as fresh herbs, or onion and garlic) process them all together to save time.

COMBINING INGREDIENTS

Forks, spoons, whisks, spatulas, manual beaters, and electric mixers are just a few of the many utensils used to combine ingredients. Here's a helpful glossary:
Blend—Combine ingredients, usually until smooth, less vigorously than beating.
Beat—Mix ingredients thoroughly and *quickly* by hand or electric mixer to a smooth, creamy texture.
Stir—Blend in a circular motion with a spoon.
Mix—Stir ingredients by hand with a spoon or fork.
Fold—Combine ingredients by lifting from underneath with a spatula. Usually used to blend a fragile mixture with a heavier one . . . like beaten egg whites and cake batter.

COOKING METHODS

There are two basic ways to cook meat, poultry, and fish—dry-heat cooking and moist-heat cooking. All recipes use one of these techniques in some form or manner, although other aspects of the recipe may mask the underlying technique. Dry-heat methods (roasting, baking, broiling, sautéing, and pan broiling) are used for the more tender cuts of meat. Moist-heat methods (braising, stewing, and simmering/poaching) are generally used with less-tender cuts. Poaching in particular, however, is often used to cook delicate pieces of chicken or fish more gently.
Each technique is briefly described below.

Roasting: Meat or poultry cooked uncovered on a rack in a shallow pan at 325° to 350°. No liquid is added. Use a meat thermometer to ensure that the food is cooked to the desired doneness. Use tongs, two large spoons, or spatulas rather than a fork to turn food so that juices are not lost.

Grilling: Cooking and browning over glowing coals, either charcoal, wood, or gas, instead of under a broiler. Outdoor cooking times can vary considerably depending on the amount of coals used and the wind and temperature.

Pan Broiling: Cooking and browning meat in a preheated heavy skillet, uncovered, with no oil or liquid. Cook slowly until nicely browned, turning frequently with tongs; pour off fat as it accumulates. To brown effectively, food should be dry, so first rub surface with a paper towel.

Sautéing: Cooking uncovered in a skillet in a small amount of oil over medium heat. Add food only when oil is hot. Turn frequently until nicely browned on all sides. This method is similar to pan broiling except that a small amount oil (or oil and butter) is used.

Stir-frying: An Oriental cooking method in which small pieces of meat, chicken, vegetables, etc., are quickly cooked in oil over high heat while continuously stirring. Traditionally done in a wok, but a large, heavy skillet will do as well.

Simmering: Cooking in a liquid just below the boiling point. (Bubbles rise occasionally to break the surface.)

Boiling: Cooking in a liquid in which bubbles rise continually and break on the surface. (At sea level, the boiling temperature of water is 210°.)

Braising: Cooking food slowly in a small amount of liquid in tightly covered cookware. For a fricassee or pot roast, the food is first browned in a little oil, the fat is poured off, and the meat is then simmered in liquid on top of the stove or in the oven until tender. This is an excellent way to cook pork or veal chops, as well as less tender steaks and roasts.

Stewing/Cooking in Liquid: Simmering for a long period in liquid in a covered casserole or Dutch oven. In most cases, the meat or poultry is browned first in a little oil or fat, then covered with a liquid—either water, stock, wine, beer, or some combination of these—and cooked until tender. Vegetables—particularly onions, celery, or carrots—and seasonings are often added to the cooking liquid. Like braising, stewing can be done either in the oven or on top of the stove.

Poaching: Simmering in liquid in a tightly covered pan until tender. Chicken parts (particularly breasts) and fish are frequently poached, usually in stock or water or a combination of wine and stock. The liquid should simmer gently so that the food, especially fish, will hold its shape during cooking.

Steaming: Cooking food in steam above boiling water using a rack or wire basket inside a large covered pot. This is particularly effective for poultry, shellfish, and vegetables.

Parboiling: Partial cooking of meat, poultry, fish, or vegetables in boiling liquid. Cooking is then continued through baking, broiling, or sautéing.

Hot-Water Bath (Bain-Marie): A hot-water bath is used in oven baking to keep delicate foods like eggs, custards, sauces, or timbales from cracking or curdling. The pan holding the food is placed in a larger pan of hot water that reaches halfway up the food container.

Using a Microwave

The microwave oven is not merely a device for defrosting and reheating, as many people seem to think. It cooks a variety of foods especially well. Because there are cooking techniques unique to the microwave, you should carefully follow the instruction book that comes with your oven.

The biggest difference between using a microwave and the standard oven is, of course, the cooking time. Remember, most microwave-cooked food also requires standing time after removal from the oven and before eating. The food continues to cook during this period. Recipes written for the microwave will indicate the amount of standing time needed.

There are other differences as well. You must use microwave-compatible cookware, of which there is a great variety available. Some can be used on the range top or under the broiler as well.

The most efficient microwave cooking vessel is round—to let food cook more evenly. In microwave cooking, the arrangement of food in a container is also important. Spread individual pieces of food apart to expose food surfaces. Arrange smaller pieces that will cook more quickly in the center; put larger ones that will take longer to cook on the outside where they will absorb more microwaves. Individual pieces of food, such as baked potatoes, should be arranged in a circle or ring around the edge of the container. To ensure even, thorough cooking, rotate or stir large quantities of food halfway through the cooking cycle.

If you normally cover a food while cooking the conventional way—steamed vegetables, for example—cover it in the microwave, too. Use glass covers whenever possible to avoid the risk of softened plastic wrap touching the food. If you don't have a proper lid, cover a microwaveable bowl with a glass lid from a casserole dish, or use a glass pie plate or microwaveable dinner plate.

Thanks to the microwave, leftovers have lost their "bad" reputation. The microwave reheats foods beautifully and quickly without loss of flavor or texture. Efficient containers available today have tight-fitting storage lids and can go from the refrigerator to the microwave to save both time and space.

Helpful Microwave Hints

- Preheat liquid for deglazing or scraping up the brown bits from a pan in which meat has been cooked. Likewise, add microwave-heated liquid to a casserole that is already cooking.
- Preheat stock, water, milk, or cream before adding to a sauce; it will thicken more quickly. *Note*: thickening sauce in the microwave is virtually foolproof.
- Sauté vegetables in a minimum amount of butter or oil in the microwave. They'll be lower in calories and retain more of their bright color than when cooked on the stove top.
- Braise meats such as pot roast or corned beef. You will need about one-third less liquid than with conventional cooking. With glass or ceramic pans you can brown meat on the stove top, then finish cooking in the microwave without changing pans. Just pour off the excess fat, add a little liquid, and cover with a glass lid.
- Partially cook ribs and chicken in the microwave, then transfer to the grill for final cooking. To avoid bacteria contamination, take the food directly from the microwave to the hot grill. (Partially cooked foods should never be left standing too long.)
- Soften cream cheese, butter, or margarine for easier, quicker use in recipes. Likewise, melt butter, margarine, chocolate, or marshmallows.
- Warm syrups, honey, refrigerated dressings, crystallized jams. *Safety note:* Never warm any of these—or any food—in narrow-necked bottles or containers. Always put the sauces, etc., in custard cups, bowls, or other open, microwaveable containers.
- Add only a little water to foods that have high water content, e.g., vegetables; too much water will slow the cooking time and leach away the vegetable's natural color and nutrients.
- Foods high in sugar, e.g., frosting or jelly, cook very quickly; watch the timing carefully.
- Allow extra cooking time for food straight from the refrigerator or below room temperature.

TRIMMING FAT AND CHOLESTEROL

Besides today's many low-fat and nonfat substitutes, there are dozens of new lower-fat cooking methods that you can follow. Some are already included in this book. If you're concerned about fat and cholesterol intake, here are some tips for adapting recipes for healthy cooking.

Sautéing Tips

- When sautéing in oil, margarine, or butter, minimize the amount by applying it with a pastry brush. Better yet, try a little nonstick cooking spray.
- A pan with a good nonstick coating will help "stretch" the small amount of fat that you use.
- Stir-fry vegetables in small amounts of chicken, beef, or vegetable stock. *Note*: The stock will never get as hot as fat, so you may have to cook the vegetables a little longer.
- Whether sautéing in a little oil, nonstick spray, or stock, cover the pan, lower the heat, and

"steam" vegetables in their own juices until soft. This will help prevent sticking and cut the need for more oil (adding more stock is fine).

Soup and Stew Tips

• Use fat-free canned chicken or beef stock, or stock that you make from dehydrated bouillon cubes (*note*: these can be salty; so look for low-sodium varieties).

• Defat soups and stocks (even canned broth) by refrigerating them thoroughly. When chilled, the fat rises to the surface, solidifies, and can easily be skimmed off.

• It's not essential to sauté garlic, onions, celery, or other vegetables when they will be cooked for several hours as in a soup. They'll soften just fine when added raw and given enough time to cook and develop their own flavors.

• Nonfat thickeners that you can use in soups or stews include: a few tablespoons of farina (Cream of Wheat), grated or pureed potato, rice, legumes, or vegetables.

Meat Tips

• When a recipe calls for sautéed ground beef, drain off the fat after cooking the meat.

• Substitute ground turkey for some of the ground beef in meatballs or meat loaf; season as usual.

• Before cooking, trim all visible fat from meat; with chicken, remove large pieces of fat from beneath skin. Poultry skin can generally be removed before cooking for all methods except oven baking or roasting. For healthy eating, remove the skin from chicken or turkey before serving.

• Fat is often what makes meat juicy. For a moist, low-fat roast, coat a lean, fat-trimmed cut of meat with a little vegetable oil, then slow-roast on a rack at a lower temperature, basting frequently with drippings.

Gravies and Sauces

• A key reason that fats are used in cooking is to intensify flavor. But delicious fat-free sauces can be made from pan juices boiled down to make them thicker and more flavorful. When making sauces with less fat, use herbs a little more freely for better flavor.

• To make a nonfat traditional-style gravy, remove fat from pan juices, then thicken the defatted juices with a little flour mixed in buttermilk or a little cornstarch mixed in water.

• Use low-fat or nonfat evaporated milk for thick, rich-tasting "cream" sauces or gravies.

Substitutions

• Recipes can often be made more healthy by substituting lower-fat or lower-cholesterol ingredients without sacrificing taste or texture. Rich dishes can be "lightened" in a number of ways.

Sour Cream, Mayonnaise, and Yogurt

• Instead of regular sour cream in a dip or dressing, use fat- or butterfat-free sour cream or even plain, low-fat or nonfat yogurt. Yogurt isn't quite as thick, but that usually doesn't matter. Even a sour-cream "half-and-half"—made of nonfat yogurt and sour cream—will trim fat and cholesterol. *Note:* In choosing a sour-cream substitute, make sure that it does not contain tropical oils, like palm or coconut oil, which are highly saturated fats.

• Substitutes generally work fine even for dishes that call for heated sour cream. In substituting plain yogurt for sour cream, keep it from separating by mixing 1 tablespoon of yogurt with 1 tablespoon of cornstarch, then mix this combination into the rest of the yogurt before heating.

• Use a low-fat, nonfat or low-cholesterol mayonnaise; or use half mayonnaise and half plain yogurt . . . the yogurt will also perk up the taste.

• *Note*: Some low-fat yogurts contain more fat than others; check the labels.

• A low-fat substitute that's great in creamy salad dressings is buttermilk; it has a lovely tang.

• Make your own mock sour cream: Add 1 cup low-fat cottage cheese to ⅛ cup nonfat yogurt or nonfat buttermilk and mix in a blender. Or blend 1 tablespoon vinegar with 1 cup yogurt.

Cream and Milk

- Fat makes heavy cream thicker than light cream. Light cream (or evaporated low-fat or nonfat milk) can be substituted for heavy cream in all recipes except those that require whipping the cream.
- Whole milk can generally be used in place of light cream.
- Instead of topping a dessert with whipped cream, try a lower-fat sour-cream substitute with a little brown sugar mixed into it.

Butter and Oils

- Using margarine instead of butter cuts down on cholesterol and often saturated fat as well.
- Although some people notice a difference in the taste of baked goods made with margarine, that's not generally true of recipes containing cocoa, chocolate, or other strong flavors.
- *Note: Diet* margarines contain water, so they can't be substituted for equal amounts of butter when baking. Nor are they ideal for sautéing.
- In baking, substitute ⅔ cup vegetable oil for each cup of butter or shortening. The texture will be somewhat different, but you'll eliminate saturated fat and use less fat overall.
- Substituting applesauce or other pureed fruit for some of the fat when baking muffins or tea breads increases moisture and flavor.
- Sauté in olive oil, vegetable oil, or regular margarine instead of butter to cut down on cholesterol. *Note:* Don't allow margarine to get so hot that it turns brown; it will take on an unpleasant flavor.
- Use margarine with as little saturated fat in it as possible, or margarine made from liquid rather than partially hydrogenated oils (hydrogenation, the process by which liquid oil is converted to solid, makes the oil more saturated).
- Use the "best" (i.e., monounsaturated) oils, olive oil, canola oil, and almond oil, whenever possible. Avoid the "worst" (saturated): palm oil, coconut oil, and palm-kernel oil.

Cheese

- Instead of whole-milk ricotta, try one of the low-fat or nonfat versions, or a low-fat or nonfat cottage cheese.
- Yogurt Cheese (see recipe p. 20) is a low-fat or nonfat substitute for cream cheese.
- Neufchatel cheese, marketed as "light" cream cheese, reduces fat and cholesterol without sacrificing taste.
- Use reduced-fat hard cheese, like Cheddar or Colby. They generally melt well, too. *Note:* Read the labels on these and on reduced-cholesterol cheeses; don't assume that "low-fat" also means "low-cholesterol," or vice versa.
- Make your own mock cream cheese by blending ½ cup uncreamed cottage cheese with 1 tablespoon plain yogurt.

Eggs

- Substitute two egg whites for each whole egg when making baked goods that call for one or two eggs. *Note:* This won't work for multiple-egg recipes like soufflés.
- Cholesterol-free liquid egg substitutes work well in pancakes, french toast, and many baked goods.

Chocolate

- Baking chocolate is high in fat but has no cholesterol; milk chocolate is high in both fat *and* cholesterol. Use cocoa whenever possible to significantly reduce fat and cholesterol.

Broths

- Beef and chicken broth are both available in fat-free varieties. Also, you can prepare most recipes with half broth and half water.
- Wine is a flavorful nonfat substitute for most recipes calling for beef or chicken broth.

For more information on fat and cholesterol, Fat and Cholesterol Charts for Dairy Foods, and other health concerns, see pages 173-179.

APPETIZERS

Appetizers and hors d'oeuvres are traditionally served to whet the appetite before a meal or as "finger foods" at a cocktail party. But these tasty delicacies are far more versatile than that. Many of the recipes in this chapter can be transformed into side dishes or even used to spark up the main dish of a meal. For example, Cornelius's Caponata, one of our favorites, can be used as a filling for omelets or as a sauce over meat for a rustic supper dish. Marinated Cauliflower is an excellent accompaniment to a picnic; leftover Cocktail Chicken Wings can form the basis of a light lunch. Yogurt Cheese has so many uses that we can't possibly name them all (although we've given you a few ideas to start with). Use your imagination!

CRUDITÉS

Crudités, raw or blanched vegetables or fruits, are universally popular—and healthy, too! But don't feel constrained to use only the old standbys that are trotted out at party after party. Why not try some of the following with your favorite dips and sauces?

Apple slices   Red cabbage, crisp slices
Beet slices   Tiny new potatoes, steamed and sliced
Daikon radish slices   Snow peas, blanched
Jicama slices   Sugar snap peas, blanched
Pear slices

In addition to the vinaigrettes, sauces, and dips provided in this book, it's easy to create your own. For instance:

● Mayonnaise blended with a little curry powder goes well with chilled artichokes and asparagus.
● Yogurt blended with lemon juice and finely chopped mint is a zesty dip for cucumbers, green beans, and carrot strips.
● Chopped fresh tomatoes mixed with pesto makes an Italian salsa that enlivens jicama, zucchini, and potato rounds.

GINGER-LIME VINAIGRETTE WITH CRUDITÉS

Use as a dip for aspargaus, green beans, broccoli, carrots, cauliflower, daikon, snow peas, or zucchini. Serve as a dressing for artichokes.

INGREDIENTS:
¼ cup grated fresh ginger
4 scallions, white and tender greens, minced
½ cup fresh lime juice
¼ cup light sesame oil
¼ cup soy sauce
¾ cup vegetable oil
Toasted sesame seeds (optional)

EQUIPMENT:
Small (1-quart) mixing bowl

Combine all ingredients except sesame seeds in bowl and whisk together. Refrigerate overnight. Add toasted sesame seeds just before serving or serve separately in a saucer in which the moistened vegetables can be dipped. **Yield: about 2 cups.**

Ginger-Lime Vinaigrette with Crudités

CURRY DIP FOR CRUDITÉS

Less fat and tastier than a mayonnaise-based dip, serve it with crudités, cold artichoke, or asparagus.

INGREDIENTS:
8 ounces farmer's cheese
¼ cup nonfat buttermilk
1 tablespoon fresh lemon juice
1 small onion, minced
1 garlic clove, minced
1 tablespoon curry powder
1 teaspoon chili powder

EQUIPMENT:
Food processor or blender

Process the farmer's cheese, buttermilk, and lemon juice in food processor or blender until smooth. Add remaining ingredients and process until well blended. Chill overnight to blend flavors. **Yield: about 1 cup.** ● ■

TIP: To smooth the curry-powder flavor, mix it with lemon juice in a glass cup and microwave on MEDIUM power for 30 seconds. Let cool before adding to processor.

HERBED OLIVES

INGREDIENTS:
½ cup olive oil
1 tablespoon red-wine vinegar
1 tablespoon chopped garlic
1 tablespoon chopped fresh rosemary leaves or
    1½ teaspoons dried rosemary
Freshly ground black pepper to taste
2 pounds large Greek olives, black and green

EQUIPMENT:
Large (4-quart) glass or ceramic bowl

Combine first five ingredients in bowl, mix well, add olives, and toss until well coated. Cover and marinate for at least 24 hours, stirring occasionally. Serve at room temperature. **Yield: about 6 cups.**

TIP: Olives will keep refrigerated for several weeks.

COCKTAIL CHICKEN WINGS

Slow cooking infuses the chicken with the flavor of its sauce.

INGREDIENTS:
36 chicken wings, rinsed
1 cup soy sauce
½ cup sugar
1 cup firmly packed dark brown sugar

EQUIPMENT:
Deep roasting pan
Small (1-quart) mixing bowl

TIP: If you reduce this recipe by half, you'll need more sauce to allow for basting and long cooking time. Make a half recipe with ⅔ cup soy sauce, ⅓ cup granulated sugar, and ⅔ cup brown sugar.

Preheat oven to 325°. The chicken is easier to eat if you cut the wing in two pieces—at the joint—and remove the wing tip. Arrange wings in a single layer in roasting pan. Combine soy sauce and sugars in bowl and mix well. Pour mixture over chicken and place pan on the middle rack of oven. Turn chicken after 30 minutes; cook an additional 30 minutes. Baste wings with the juices and cook for a final 20 minutes. Serve warm or at room temperature. **Yield: 72 pieces.**

Antipasto Platter

ANTIPASTO PLATTER

INGREDIENTS:
4 red bell peppers
1 pound fresh mozzarella cheese, sliced
4 fresh tomatoes, sliced, or 12 sun-dried
   tomatoes, halved
1 tablespoon extra-virgin olive oil
8 to 12 fresh basil leaves, chopped
1 pound prosciutto, very thinly sliced
1 honeydew melon or cantaloupe, cut in 2-inch
   wedges, *or* 8 fresh figs, peeled, halved, or
   quartered
Juice of 1 to 2 lemons
Salt and freshly ground black pepper to taste

EQUIPMENT:
Glass bowl

Preheat oven to Broil. Halve the peppers lengthwise and remove core, seeds, and stem. Place them skin-side up on a foil-lined broiler pan. Turn during broiling and evenly blacken skins. Place peppers in a large glass bowl, cover, and let them steam 10 minutes before removing skin.

On a large platter, arrange alternate slices of mozzarella cheese and tomato; drizzle with olive oil and sprinkle with basil, salt, and pepper. Circle with slices of prosciutto-wrapped melon or place figs on top of prosciutto. Circle again with roasted peppers; drizzle with lemon juice and pepper. Serve at room temperature. **Serves 12 to 16.**

CORNELIUS'S CAPONATA

Serve as an appetizer with crisp crackers or use as a filling for omelets or crepes. Dusted with freshly shredded Parmesan cheese, it makes a great luncheon dish. Add Italian sausages and squares of polenta for a festive supper dish.

INGREDIENTS:
¼ cup olive oil
1 medium eggplant, peeled and diced
1 cup chopped onion
1 garlic clove, chopped
1 green or red bell pepper, seeded, cored, and
 chopped
½ cup minced celery
1 cup canned or fresh tomato puree
⅓ cup chopped pitted green olives
2 tablespoons capers, rinsed and drained
2 tablespoons red-wine or cider vinegar
1 tablespoon sugar
Freshly ground black pepper to taste
2 tablespoons chopped fresh Italian flat-leaf
 parsley
¼ cup shredded Parmesan cheese (optional)

EQUIPMENT:
2½-quart covered saucepan

Heat 3 tablespoons of the oil in saucepan over medium heat. Add eggplant and cook, stirring occasionally until eggplant is almost translucent, about 10 minutes. Add remaining olive oil, onion, garlic, peppers, and celery. Cook, stirring, until onion is limp, about 10 minutes. Add tomato puree, olives, capers, vinegar, and sugar. Sprinkle lightly with a few grinds of pepper; stir gently to combine. Cover and simmer, stirring occasionally, for 30 minutes to 1 hour until very thick; add water only if necessary. Taste and add more seasonings if needed. Stir in parsley. Let cool, then refrigerate until used. Serve with crackers, bread, or melba toast. **Yield: about 3 cups.**

YOGURT AIOLI

This flavorful variation of a traditional aioli relies on garlic that is baked for over an hour to develop a nutty sweet taste. The dip requires very little hands-on time but considerable standing time to let flavors blend, so make it at least 6 hours before serving. Serve with crudités.

INGREDIENTS:
1 small head garlic
1 to 2 teaspoons olive oil
2 cups plain yogurt
1 cup mayonnaise
1 tablespoon minced fresh chives

EQUIPMENT:
Small baking dish or small ramekin
Small (1-quart) mixing bowl

Preheat oven to 350°. Keeping garlic head intact, remove the loose outer papery skin. Cut off tip of head to just expose the cloves and place in baking dish. Coat with oil. Pour a little olive oil and water into the dish and bake about 1¼ hours, until very soft and tender. Allow to cool. Squeeze cloves out of their skin. Place in a bowl and mash; add remaining ingredients and blend well. Refrigerate at least 6 hours before serving. **Yield: 3 cups.**

> TO PEEL GARLIC easily and minimize contact with your skin, place unpeeled garlic cloves in the microwave and cook on HIGH for 10 seconds. Trim the root end of the clove with a sharp knife and the garlic will pop right out of its skin.

New Potatoes with Dill

NEW POTATOES WITH DILL

INGREDIENTS:

12 small red-skinned new potatoes, scrubbed but not peeled

¼ cup sour cream or plain Yogurt Cheese (see p. 20)

Coarsely ground black pepper to taste

Chopped fresh dill for garnish

EQUIPMENT:

3-quart saucepan

Place potatoes in boiling salted water to cover. Cook 15 to 20 minutes until tender. Drain and let stand. After potatoes have cooled, slice in half. Top with a dollop of sour cream or Yogurt Cheese (see p. 20) and sprinkle with pepper and dill. Serve cold or at room temperature. **Serves 4.** ● ■

VARIATION: Top potatoes prepared as above with salmon roe or caviar.

ARTICHOKE GRATIN SPREAD

INGREDIENTS:

1 (14-ounce) can water-packed artichoke hearts, drained and chopped

½ cup grated Parmesan cheese

1 cup mayonnaise

1 garlic clove, minced

Dash cayenne pepper or hot sauce

EQUIPMENT:

Medium (2½-quart) mixing bowl

8-inch square baking pan

Preheat oven to 350°. Mix all ingredients together in bowl, then place in pan. Bake 20 minutes, or until brown and bubbly. Serve warm with crackers. **Serves 6.**

VARIATION: Spread on crackers and top with a small dollop of mayonnaise blended with curry powder.

Cucumber Yogurt and *Hummus* with pita bread

HUMMUS WITH TOASTED PITA

INGREDIENTS:
¼ cup tahini (sesame paste)
⅓ cup fresh lemon juice
⅓ to ½ cup warm water, as needed
2 garlic cloves, chopped
1 (16-ounce) can chick peas, drained, rinsed with
   cold water, and drained again
Salt and freshly ground white or black pepper to
   taste
Extra-virgin olive oil and/or chopped fresh
   parsley for garnish (optional)
Toasted pita bread

EQUIPMENT:
Food processor or blender
Refrigerator storage container

Process tahini, lemon juice, ⅓ cup water, and garlic in food processor or blender until smooth. With food processor running, gradually add chick peas, salt, and pepper, processing until mixture is a very thick paste. (If using a blender, add chick peas in ¼ cup batches.) The hummus will continue to thicken in the refrigerator, so if it seems too thick add more water and process again.

Place hummus in a covered container and refrigerate for up to a week; it can also be frozen. Before serving, drizzle with olive oil and garnish with chopped parsley, if desired. Serve with toasted pita wedges. **Yield: about 2 cups.**

TIP: Tahini, a paste made from sesame seeds, is often used in Middle Eastern recipes and can be found in shops specializing in Middle Eastern foods, or check the gourmet section of your supermarket for tins of sesame paste.

CUCUMBER YOGURT AND PITA

For a nice contrast of flavors, serve this appetizer with Hummus (see p. 18) or with a smoked-fish platter.

INGREDIENTS:
1 cup plain yogurt
1 garlic clove, minced (optional)
1 tablespoon minced fresh dill or 1½ teaspoons dried dill weed
2 teaspoons white-wine vinegar
Salt to taste
2 cucumbers, peeled, seeded, and finely chopped
Pita bread

EQUIPMENT:
Medium (2½-quart) mixing bowl

Place all ingredients except cucumber and pita bread in bowl and mix well with fork or whisk. Add cucumber and mix again. Cover and refrigerate at least 2 hours before serving. Serve chilled with toasted pita bread. As a cucumber salad to accompany a spicy main course, slice cucumbers instead of chopping. **Yield: about 2 cups.**

PARTY PECANS

INGREDIENTS:
2 teaspoons each ground cumin, chili powder, and garlic pepper
1 teaspoon each ground ginger, cinnamon, and cayenne pepper
6 tablespoons olive oil
8 cups pecan halves

EQUIPMENT:
Large (4-quart) mixing bowl
8-inch sauté pan
Baking sheet

Preheat oven to 325°. Mix spices together in bowl. Heat olive oil in sauté pan over low heat. Add spices, mix well, and simmer 3 minutes. Add pecans to bowl, pour spice and oil mixture over, and toss well. Spread pecans in a single layer on baking sheet and bake 15 minutes. Repeat until all the nuts are baked. Return pecans (and any stray crumbs left on the baking sheet) to bowl and toss again. Cover and set aside at least 2 hours before serving. **Yield: 8 cups.**

MARINATED CAULIFLOWER

INGREDIENTS:
1 medium head cauliflower, about 3 pounds, cored and broken into florets
⅔ cup water
⅔ cup red-wine vinegar
1 tablespoon sugar
1 garlic clove, minced
12 to 16 fresh basil leaves, chopped
1 teaspoon finely chopped fresh chives
Salt and freshly ground black pepper to taste

EQUIPMENT:
3-quart covered saucepan with steamer
1-quart saucepan
Medium (2½ quart) bowl

Steam cauliflower florets 5 minutes. Remove florets from steamer and place in bowl or storage container. Reserve water (add more if necessary to make ⅔ cup). Whisk together water, vinegar, sugar, and garlic in smaller saucepan. Bring to a boil; remove from heat and add basil, chives, salt, and pepper. Allow liquid to cool before pouring over florets. Cover and refrigerate at least 3 hours. Drain before serving. **Yield: about 4 cups.**

Herbed Yogurt Cheese Dip

YOGURT CHEESE AND DIPS

This is a good low-fat or nonfat alternative to cream cheese. Use as you would cream cheese—plain, with chopped vegetables, with raisins and walnuts, with minced smoked salmon—or in one of the variations below.

INGREDIENTS:

1 quart plain low-fat or nonfat yogurt, without agar or gelatin

EQUIPMENT:

Medium (2½-quart) mixing bowl
Large sieve and tea towel, or yogurt funnel

TIP: Be sure towel is clean—freshly washed and rinsed thoroughly to remove all traces of soap, detergents, bleach, or fabric softener.

Line sieve with towel. Place sieve or yogurt funnel over bowl, allowing at least a 1-inch space at bottom of bowl for liquid to drain and collect. Spoon yogurt into sieve or funnel. If using sieve, twist towel closed and fasten with clip or clothespin. If using yogurt funnel, cover loosely with plastic wrap. Place in refrigerator and allow liquid to drain until Yogurt Cheese is of desired consistency (8 to 14 hours or more). The longer the Yogurt Cheese drains, the firmer it will get. **Yield: about 1¼ cups.** ● ■

HERBED YOGURT CHEESE SPREAD

INGREDIENTS:

1 tablespoon chopped fresh herbs, singly or in combination: thyme, tarragon, and chervil
2 garlic cloves, very finely minced
Parsley for garnish, finely chopped

Add herbs and garlic to Yogurt Cheese. Mix well and refrigerate at least 1 hour to blend flavors. Sprinkle with parsley before serving. Serve at room temperature as a spread for crackers or crusty bread, or thin with some of the whey (liquid from Yogurt Cheese) and use as a dip. ● ■

SOUTHWESTERN YOGURT CHEESE SPREAD

INGREDIENTS:

½ teaspoon ground cumin
2 garlic cloves, finely minced
1 jalapeño pepper, seeded and minced
1 mild green canned chili, chopped
1 tablespoon chopped fresh cilantro

Mix all ingredients with Yogurt Cheese and refrigerate at least 1 hour to blend flavors. Serve at room temperature as a spread on jicama slices or on toasted tortilla pieces. Thin with whey to desired consistency for use as a dip with chips. ● ■

ITALIAN –STYLE YOGURT CHEESE SPREAD

INGREDIENTS:

6 to 8 sun-dried tomato halves, finely chopped
½ teaspoon freshly ground white pepper
3 tablespoons chopped fresh basil leaves
1 to 2 garlic cloves, minced

Mix all ingredients with Yogurt Cheese and refrigerate for at least 1 hour to blend flavors. Serve at room temperature as a spread on hot, toasted Italian bread, bread sticks, or plain focaccia bread. ● ■

TIP: Truly dry "sun-dried" tomatoes (those *not* packed in oil), need to be reconstituted in warm water, then drained before use.

Yogurt Cheese

SEVICHE

The traditional form of this recipe uses raw scallops. In this version, however, the scallops are cooked before marinating.

INGREDIENTS:

1 cup bay scallops (small) or sea scallops (large), about ½ pound, cut into bite-size pieces
⅔ cup water
½ cup fresh lime juice
2 tablespoons finely chopped onion
2 tablespoons finely chopped parsley
1 tablespoon finely chopped green bell pepper
1 tablespoon finely chopped red bell pepper
¼ cup finely chopped fresh tomatoes
4 tablespoons extra-virgin olive oil
Pinch of cayenne
Salt and freshly ground black pepper to taste
Fresh cilantro leaves for garnish (optional)

EQUIPMENT:

2½-quart covered saucepan
2½-quart glass or ceramic shallow bowl

Place scallops in simmering water, cover, and simmer 3 to 5 minutes. Drain and put in shallow bowl, cover with lime juice, and refrigerate overnight. When ready to serve, combine scallops with remaining ingredients and mix well. **Yield: about 3 cups.**

TIPS: If you like your seviche spicy, substitute 1 small jalapeño pepper, seeded and finely diced, for the green bell pepper.

You may substitute any firm-fleshed white fish for the scallops.

SALADS

The popularity of salads is much deserved. The variety of flavors, nutritional value, and ease of preparation make a salad the perfect dish for today's life-style. Greens should be included with every meal—and can even be a meal in themselves! So always make generous amounts of salad—leftovers can be turned into a quick gazpacho.

In Europe, green salads are traditionally served after the main course. Californians like to serve the salad in a big bowl on the table from the start of a meal so that one can eat salad from the first course through the last. Luncheons composed of a large salad and a small portion of meat, poultry, fish, or cheese are a healthy repast.

Creamy mayonnaise-based dressings, once so popular, were probably developed to add flavor to otherwise-bland greens such as iceberg lettuce. Thanks to modern farm technology and shipping methods, however, bland, tasteless greens are a thing of the past. So skip the mayonnaise dressing—replace it with yogurt or vinaigrette—and enjoy *healthy*, flavorful salads.

Be adventurous. Create your own salads and dressings—we have provided you with some basic vinaigrette starters—and enjoy a salad before, during, or after the main course.

A SELECT SAMPLING OF GREENS

Arugula—Dark green leaves with pungent, peppery flavor that are delicious on their own or combined with milder lettuce.

Belgian endive—Whitish (or a newly popular red version), crisp leaves that are slightly bitter and combine well with a variety of lettuces.

Bibb, Boston, butterhead lettuce—Small pale leaves, slightly crunchy and sweet; appealing with citrus dressings.

Curly endive or chicory—Tart and crunchy, these are best when young and used in moderation.

Dandelion greens—Tart and slightly acid, these slender green leaves with a soft texture become more pungent (and darker) as they age.

Escarole—Although tart, this green is less bitter than curly endive; best served alone.

Field lettuce (mache)—This fall/winter green has small, green leaves and a sweet-nutty flavor.

Frisee—This is the sweetest of the chicory family, although still bitter; try it with arugula.

Loose-leaf lettuce—Red or green leaves, delicately flavored. These combine well with a variety of more pungent greens.

Radicchio—Ruby red and peppery; try it with a robust dressing.

Romaine—These crisp green leaves have a nutty flavor and can be used with most other greens.

Sorrel—With a lemony sour taste, this green should be used sparingly.

Watercress—These peppery/spicy small dark green leaves are wonderful alone or mixed with other greens. They are packed with nutritional value: watercress has twice the protein and four times the vitamin C of lettuce.

Winter Holiday Salad , see p. 24.

WINTER HOLIDAY SALAD

Adding the dressing ahead of time lets the watercress wilt slightly and blends flavors nicely. It's a perfect make-ahead dish for the holiday chef who wants to spend more time with family and guests.

INGREDIENTS:
2 small heads red cabbage, cored and coarsely chopped
4 bunches watercress, coarsely chopped
2 heads Belgian endive, base trimmed and coarsely chopped
12 scallions, white and tender greens, chopped
2 red or Granny Smith apples, unpeeled, cored, and sliced
8 ounces Stilton cheese, crumbled
Dressing:
1 cup walnut oil
⅓ cup red-wine, raspberry, or cider vinegar
Salt and freshly ground black pepper to taste

EQUIPMENT:
Salad bowl
Small bowl or 2-cup measuring cup

Toss all salad ingredients together in salad bowl. Whisk together oil and vinegar; add salt and pepper to taste; pour dressing over salad and refrigerate at least 1 hour before serving. **Serves 8.**

See photo, p. 22.

WARM GOAT-CHEESE SALAD

INGREDIENTS:
1 small head Boston lettuce
1 small head radicchio
1 small head red leaf lettuce
1 (4-ounce) log firm, sharp goat cheese, preferably Montrachet
Vinaigrette:
1¼ cups walnut or olive oil
⅓ cup red-wine vinegar
1 tablespoon finely chopped shallots
Salt and freshly ground black pepper to taste
Garlic Croutons:
⅓ baguette (a long, thin loaf of French bread)
¼ cup olive oil
1 garlic clove, cut in half
Fresh parsley for garnish

EQUIPMENT:
Medium (2½-quart) mixing bowl
8-inch square baking dish

Tear lettuces into bite-sized pieces and mix together in medium bowl. To make the vinaigrette, whisk the oil into the vinegar and add shallots, salt, and pepper. Reserve 2 tablespoons of vinaigrette, pour the remainder over the lettuce and toss. Distribute evenly on 4 dinner plates.

Preheat oven to Broil. To make croutons, cut baguette crosswise into 16 equal slices about ¼ inch thick. Toast under broiler on both sides until golden brown. Remove from broiler, brush both sides with olive oil and rub with cut garlic clove.

Lower oven temperature to 400°. Cut goat cheese crosswise into 4 equal slices. Flatten by hand into rounds and place in baking dish. Drizzle a little of the reserved vinaigrette over each and place in the hot oven for about 1 minute until cheese is slightly browned and melted. Place 1 piece of warm goat cheese on each salad, garnish each with 4 croutons and parsley, and serve immediately. **Serves 4.**

Minted Cucumber

MINTED CUCUMBER

This delightful accompaniment to beef dishes is also terrific with spicy foods.

INGREDIENTS:
1 tablespoon sugar
1 cup warm water
1 cup white-wine vinegar
Salt and freshly ground white pepper to taste
1 long seedless cucumber, peeled and sliced very
 thin
½ cup chopped mint leaves

EQUIPMENT:
Bowl or refrigerator storage container

In bowl, dissolve sugar in warm water; add water and vinegar. Whisk and add mint and cucumbers. Cover and refrigerate at least 3 hours, but not more than 6. Drain cucumbers before serving. **Serves 6.** ● ■

GREEN BEAN SALAD

INGREDIENTS:
1½ pounds green beans
1 medium red onion, thinly sliced
6 tablespoons olive oil
1 teaspoon sugar
3 tablespoons finely chopped fresh dill
Salt and freshly ground black pepper to taste
2 tablespoons red-wine vinegar

EQUIPMENT:
2-quart covered saucepan with steamer
Colander
Bowl or refrigerator storage container
Small bowl or 2-cup measuring cup

Steam green beans just until tender-crisp, then place immediately in colander under cold running water for 2 minutes to stop cooking. Combine beans and sliced onion in salad bowl or refrigerator storage container. Thoroughly mix remaining ingredients, except vinegar, and pour over vegetables, tossing lightly. Refrigerate until beans are well chilled, about 20 minutes. Just before serving, pour vinegar over beans and toss well. **Serves 6.**

VARIATION: Try preparing the salad with "homemade" tarragon vinegar (see p. 30).

See photo, p. 89.

SPINACH AND MARINATED MUSHROOM SALAD

The marinated mushrooms are healthier than the traditional bacon and hard-cooked eggs usually served in spinach salads.

INGREDIENTS:
1 cup water
1 pound small fresh mushrooms, trimmed and halved
3 large garlic cloves, mashed
1 bay leaf
½ teaspoon dried thyme
½ teaspoon dried, crushed rosemary
¼ teaspoon dried marjoram
Salt and freshly ground black pepper to taste
Juice of ½ lemon
½ cup olive oil
¾ cup wine vinegar
2 pounds spinach

EQUIPMENT:
Small bowl or 2-cup measuring cup
Salad bowl

Bring 1 cup water to a boil; add mushrooms, cover, and boil 2 minutes. Drain and place in glass bowl. Whisk together remaining ingredients except spinach in small bowl and blend well. Pour over hot mushrooms and chill at least 1 hour. Tear spinach into bite-sized pieces and place in salad bowl. Add mushrooms and enough marinade to dress, but not drown, greens. Toss lightly and serve. **Serves 8.**
● ■

INSALATA TRICOLORE

INGREDIENTS:
2 large bunches arugula, about 4 cups
2 heads radicchio
2 heads Belgian endive, base trimmed
Dressing:
3 tablespoons red-wine or balsamic vinegar
2 teaspoons Dijon-style mustard
½ cup walnut oil or extra-virgin olive oil
Salt and freshly ground black pepper to taste
1 tablespoon chopped fresh basil leaves

EQUIPMENT:
Salad bowl
Small bowl or 2-cup measuring cup

Tear arugula and radicchio into large pieces. Chop endive coarsely and toss all three lettuces in salad bowl. Whisk mustard into vinegar in bowl; add oil, salt, pepper, and basil; blend thoroughly. Pour dressing over salad and toss. **Serves 6.**

LIGHT AND CREAMY POTATO SALAD

A tangy, lower-fat version of an American classic.

INGREDIENTS:
2 pounds small new potatoes, scrubbed but not peeled
2 cups low-fat cottage cheese
2 cups low-fat or nonfat plain yogurt
2 tablespoons chopped fresh chives
1½ tablespoons Dijon-style mustard
2 tablespoons capers
Salt and freshly ground black pepper to taste

EQUIPMENT:
6-quart stockpot
Large (4-quart) mixing bowl

Place potatoes in boiling water; boil 15 to 18 minutes, or until just cooked. Be careful not to overcook. Drain and cool for several minutes until potatoes can be handled easily. Cut potatoes into generous bite-sized chunks.

Whisk together the cottage cheese and yogurt in mixing bowl. Add chives, mustard, capers, salt, and pepper and mix well. Add potato chunks to yogurt-cheese mixture. Toss well. Serve immediately, or chill an hour or so before serving. **Serves 8.** ● ■

Papaya Salad

PAPAYA SALAD

INGREDIENTS:
3 papayas, peeled, seeded, and sliced
Juice of 1 lemon
1 cup plain yogurt
¼ teaspoon thyme
Freshly ground black pepper to taste
¼ teaspoon curry powder
2 bunches watercress

EQUIPMENT:
Food processor or blender

Sprinkle papaya slices with lemon juice. Process together the yogurt, thyme, pepper, and curry powder briefly in a food processor or blender. Place papaya slices on a bed of watercress and drizzle with yogurt dressing. **Serves 6.** ● ■

TIP: To make preparation effortless, serve papaya halves, seeded but unpeeled, with dressing in the hollowed-out center. Serve with spoons so that diners can "scoop out" the papayas.

SUNFLOWER SLAW

A Jerusalem artichoke is a sunflower tuber. Affectionately called a sunchoke by many, it is appreciated for its flavor, which slightly resembles that of an artichoke although they are not in the same family.

INGREDIENTS:
1 pound Jerusalem artichokes, peeled and coarsely grated
1 yellow bell pepper, cored, seeded, and finely chopped
3 scallions, white and tender greens, chopped
½ cup plain yogurt
1 tablespoon mayonnaise
2 tablespoons fresh lemon juice
¼ teaspoon celery seed

EQUIPMENT:
Small bowl or 2-cup measuring cup
Salad bowl

Combine Jerusalem artichoke, pepper, and scallions in medium bowl. In small bowl, mix together the remaining ingredients; add to vegetables. Refrigerate to chill before serving. **Serves 6.** ● ■

COLORFUL SALAD

INGREDIENTS:
2 heads romaine lettuce
1 large red or yellow bell pepper, cored, seeded, and sliced in thin strips
1 red onion, thinly sliced in rings
1 cucumber, sliced in rounds
1 large tomato, cut in wedges
1 avocado, sliced
4 radishes, trimmed and sliced
1 bunch fresh cilantro, leaves chopped
Dressing:
3 tablespoons balsamic vinegar
½ cup olive oil
1 tablespoon Dijon-style mustard
1 garlic clove, mashed
¼ teaspoon dried, crushed marjoram or basil
Salt and freshly ground black pepper to taste

EQUIPMENT:
Small bowl or 2-cup measuring cup
Salad bowl

   Whisk dressing ingredients together in bowl. Set aside to develop flavors. Break the lettuce leaves into large pieces. Toss the rest of the salad ingredients together with lettuce in salad bowl. Remove garlic clove from the dressing. Whisk again and pour over salad just before serving. Toss salad and serve. **Serves 6.**

TIP: Add leftover salad to Gazpacho (see p. 39). Process with vegetables.

See photo, p. 74.

WARM GRECIAN CHICKEN SALAD

Don't be daunted by this main-course salad's long list of ingredients. It's simple to prepare and requires little hands-on time, although the chicken must marinate for an hour.

INGREDIENTS:
1 whole chicken breast, skinned and boned
¼ cup olive oil
4 tablespoons red-wine vinegar
2 garlic cloves, minced
1 teaspoon freshly ground black pepper
1 teaspoon dried *fines herbes*
1 cup orzo pasta
1 bunch spinach
1 red bell pepper, cored, seeded, and sliced
¼ cup imported black olives
½ small red onion, thinly sliced
¼ pound feta cheese, crumbled
Dressing:
1 teaspoon grated lemon zest
3 tablespoons fresh lemon juice
2 garlic cloves, minced
1 teaspoon white-wine vinegar
½ cup extra-virgin olive oil
Salt and freshly ground black pepper to taste

EQUIPMENT:
Glass pie plate
Small bowl or 2-cup measuring cup

   Place chicken in pie plate. Blend olive oil, vinegar, garlic, pepper, and *fines herbes* in small bowl; pour over chicken and marinate at least 1 hour before cooking.
   Cook pasta according to package directions, drain and toss with a little oil so it won't stick. Set aside 15 minutes to cool. Arrange spinach in the bottom of two large individual salad bowls. Set half the pasta in the middle of each bowl. Arrange peppers, olives, and onions alternately around the orzo, leaving a space for the chicken.
   Drain chicken and discard marinade. Grill or broil chicken breast, approximately 8 minutes on each side. Slice chicken into bite-sized ½-inch strips. Arrange chicken on spinach. Sprinkle each salad with half the feta. Whisk together dressing ingredients until well blended. Season with salt and pepper and serve separately. **Serves 2 as main course.**

Fruited Chicken Salad

FRUITED CHICKEN SALAD

WITH RASPBERRY VINAIGRETTE

INGREDIENTS:
2 whole chicken breasts, cooked
2 tart, ripe, unpeeled apples such as Granny
   Smiths, cored and cut in thin slices
1 cup small seedless green or red grapes
½ cup chopped walnuts
Red or green lettuce leaves
Vinaigrette:
⅓ cup extra-virgin olive oil
¼ cup raspberry vinegar
Salt and freshly ground black pepper to taste

EQUIPMENT:
Small bowl or 2-cup measuring cup
Medium (2½-quart) mixing bowl

To make vinaigrette, whisk together olive oil, vinegar, salt, and pepper and blend well.

Cut *cooked* chicken into bite-sized or larger pieces. Toss chicken, apple slices, grapes, and walnuts with vinaigrette. Arrange lettuce leaves on a serving plate and chicken, fruit, and nuts in the center. **Serves 4 as main course.**

TIPS: Poach chicken with skin on the bone for better flavor. After cooking, remove skin and bone.

Toast walnuts lightly in a 300° oven for about 10 minutes. Cool before using.

BASIC VINAIGRETTE

The classic proportions for vinaigrette are 3 to 4 parts oil to 1 part vinegar or citrus juice. The wide variety of vinegars and oils available today can make even the simplest vinaigrette a true taste sensation.

INGREDIENTS:
¾ cup oil: olive, vegetable, or nut
¼ cup wine, cider, or balsamic vinegar; or citrus juice
(Optional—fresh or dried herbs, spices, garlic, onion, mustard, etc.)
Salt and freshly ground black pepper to taste

Combine ingredients in a small bowl and whisk until thoroughly blended. Or shake well in a small jar with screw cap firmly in place. **Yield: 1 cup.**

DIJON VINAIGRETTE

INGREDIENTS:
⅔ cup olive oil
4 teaspoons prepared Dijon-style mustard
¼ cup red-wine vinegar
2 scallions, white and tender greens, minced
1 tablespoon fresh thyme leaves or 1 teaspoon dried thyme
Salt and freshly ground black pepper to taste

Combine as above. **Yield: about 1 cup.**

MUSTARD-DILL VINAIGRETTE

INGREDIENTS:
1 tablespoon Dijon-style mustard
3 tablespoons white-wine vinegar
¾ cup extra-virgin olive oil
2 tablespoons finely chopped fresh dill
1 small shallot, finely minced
Salt and freshly ground black pepper to taste

Combine as above. **Yield: about 1 cup.**

CITRUS VINAIGRETTE

INGREDIENTS:
⅔ cup walnut oil
1 tablespoon raspberry vinegar
2 tablespoons fresh lemon, lime, or grapefruit juice
Salt and freshly ground black pepper to taste

Combine as above. **Yield: about ¾ cup.**

GARLIC VINAIGRETTE

INGREDIENTS:
¾ cup olive oil
¼ cup red-wine vinegar
2 large garlic cloves, finely minced
Salt and freshly ground black pepper to taste

Combine as above. **Yield: about 1 cup.**

FLAVORED VINEGARS can be quite expensive, but you can easily make your own. Fill a bottle with cider vinegar or red- or white-wine vinegar, then add:
• Sprigs of fresh tarragon for tarragon vinegar
• Crushed garlic cloves for garlic vinegar
• Sprigs of fresh thyme, oregano, and rosemary for herb vinegar
Cap the bottle tightly and steep several days before using.

Tuna and Cannellini Salad

ARUGULA, GRAPEFRUIT, AND GOAT-CHEESE SALAD

INGREDIENTS:
2 large bunches arugula, about 4 cups
1 to 2 grapefruits, peeled segments
8 ounces soft goat cheese, preferably
    Montrachet or Caprini
Dressing:
¼ cup walnut or hazelnut oil
1 tablespoon safflower oil
3 tablespoons raspberry or other fruited vinegar
Salt and freshly ground black pepper to taste

EQUIPMENT:
Small bowl or 2-cup measuring cup

    Arrange arugula on individual plates. Place 4 to 6 segments of grapefruit on the arugula. Add 3 to 4 small pats of goat cheese. Whisk together oil, vinegar, and seasonings in bowl and blend well. Pour dressing over individual salads. **Serves 6.**

Arugula, Grapefruit, and Goat-Cheese Salad

TUNA AND CANNELLINI SALAD

    A quick, delicious salad that's a meal in itself when served with crusty French or Italian bread.

INGREDIENTS:
1 (20-ounce) can cannellini (white kidney beans),
    drained
3 scallions, white and tender greens, minced
2 garlic cloves, minced
½ teaspoon dried oregano
¼ teaspoon dried marjoram
1 tablespoon white-wine vinegar
2 tablespoons fresh lemon juice
⅓ cup olive oil
Salt and freshly ground black pepper to taste
2 (6⅛-ounce) cans white tuna, water packed,
    drained
2 tomatoes, quartered
8 pitted ripe olives, sliced

EQUIPMENT:
Small bowl or 2-cup measuring cup

    Place beans in serving bowl. Add scallions, garlic, herbs, vinegar, lemon juice, olive oil, salt, and pepper, and toss lightly. In small bowl, break tuna into small chunks with a fork; add to bean mixture and toss just enough to blend. Garnish with tomato wedges and ripe olives. **Serves 4 as main course.**

SOUPS AND STEWS

Soups are the answer to any busy cook's prayers—not just because they're quickly prepared, but also because most soups taste even better the next day. Always try to make soups in large quantities, refrigerating some for the next day and even freezing some for "instant" dinners, emergencies, and drop-in guests.

Because few Americans eat enough vegetables and most consume far too much meat, this chapter concentrates on vegetable soups. Some are water based; others are chicken or beef-broth based. To eliminate fat, any soup can be made with a vegetable broth. See page 10 to learn other ways of eliminating fats from soup.

For soup stock, save water in which vegetables have been blanched, boiled, or steamed. If you're not ready to use it right away, store in refrigerator or freezer. If freezing, be sure to label it.

A FINAL WORD: Whenever you have small quantities of leftovers, think of creating your own soups and stews!

VEGETABLE BROTH

INGREDIENTS:
6 quarts water
2 to 3 onions, halved
1 head celery, base trimmed, stalks cut in half
4 large carrots, cut in half
2 to 3 large leeks (optional), all but 3 inches of
   greens removed

EQUIPMENT:
8-quart covered stockpot
   Add vegetables to boiling water; reduce heat, cover, and simmer for 2 to 3 hours. Uncover and boil to reduce volume by about ¼ to ⅓ . Strain liquid, cool, and refrigerate or freeze—it will keep for several weeks in the freezer. **Yield: 4 quarts.**

● ■

SPRING VEGETABLE CHOWDER

Not every chowder has clams; this one is pure vegetable.

INGREDIENTS:
¼ cup chopped onion
½ cup chopped celery
¼ cup cored, seeded, and chopped green bell
   pepper
2 tablespoons butter or margarine
1 cup peeled and diced potatoes
2 cups water or vegetable broth (above)
Pinch dried marjoram
Pinch dried tarragon
Salt and freshly ground black pepper to taste
2 cups fresh or frozen whole kernel corn
1 cup cut green beans, in 1-inch lengths
3 tablespoons flour
3 cups milk

EQUIPMENT:
4-quart covered saucepan
Small (1-quart) mixing bowl

Spring Vegetable Chowder

   Cook onion, celery, and pepper in butter over medium heat until almost tender, stirring occasionally. Add potatoes, water, and seasonings. Cover, bring to a boil over high heat. Reduce heat to medium and simmer until potatoes are tender, about 15 minutes. Add corn and beans and simmer, covered, 10 more minutes.

   Mix flour with ¼ cup milk, then add to remaining milk and stir to blend. Pour milk mixture into vegetables and broth and cook, stirring constantly, until slightly thickened. **Serves 4 to 6.** ▼

TIP: To reduce calories and fat, omit the milk/flour mixture. Simmer the soup for an additional 30 minutes to enhance the flavor. ● ■ ▼

CURRIED GINGER-PUMPKIN SOUP

INGREDIENTS:

3 cups canned pumpkin
1 medium onion, chopped
4 to 5 cups chicken broth, canned or homemade
½ cup dry white wine
1 teaspoon grated fresh ginger
1 teaspoon curry powder
Salt and coarsely ground black pepper to taste
Finely chopped fresh chives for garnish

EQUIPMENT:

3-quart saucepan
Food processor or blender

Place canned pumpkin in saucepan with broth and onion. Cook over medium heat, stirring frequently, for 10 minutes then puree in food processor.

Return puree to saucepan; add wine, ginger, curry powder, salt, and pepper and reheat. If soup seems too thin, knead together equal amounts of butter and flour and drop into the hot puree, whisking constantly, until it reaches desired consistency. Serve in individual bowls and sprinkle with fresh chives. **Serves 6.** ● ■

TIP: Instead of canned pumpkin, you can use fresh pumpkin or winter squash. See directions, p. 97, for steaming or baking it; then add to food processor with cooked broth and onion mixture.

HEARTY MEDITERRANEAN SOUP

This soup is so full of flavor it doesn't require a meat- or vegetable-broth base, but if you prefer one, substitute full-strength or diluted broth for the water.

INGREDIENTS:

3 tablespoons olive oil
3 leeks, white parts and 1 inch of the green,
    sliced
2 red onions, thinly sliced
3 garlic cloves, minced
1½ to 2 quarts water
1 head red cabbage, cored and finely shredded
1 (8-ounce) can fava beans (or white beans)
1 teaspoon dried rosemary
8 to 10 cups shredded spinach leaves
Salt and freshly ground black pepper to taste
Toasted garlic bread with Parmesan cheese for
    garnish (optional)

EQUIPMENT:

4½-quart covered Dutch oven

Heat oil in Dutch oven over medium heat; add leeks, onions, and garlic and sauté briefly. Add water, cabbage, beans, and rosemary. Bring to a boil, cover, and simmer ½ hour; remove lid and simmer 1 more hour. Add spinach 5 minutes before serving.

You can garnish the soup with toasted garlic bread and Parmesan cheese. To prepare: Toast bread and spread with olive oil and some finely minced garlic. Sprinkle with grated Parmesan cheese and float the toast in individual soup bowls. Spoon hot soup over the bread to melt the cheese and soften the toast. **Serves 6.** ● ■ ▼

TIP: To eliminate fat entirely, skip the sautéing step and add the leeks, onions, and garlic directly to boiling water.

FARINA or instant Cream of Wheat is an excellent thickener for soups and can be used to replace potatoes and cream as thickeners. Add to soup when at a boil, reduce heat, and cook for a minimum of 5 minutes.

Miso Feast

MISO FEAST

INGREDIENTS:
6 to 8 ounces Oriental noodles, somen, udon, or
   any kind of thin noodle
3½ quarts water
1 small carrot, sliced in very thin discs
6 mushrooms, trimmed and very thinly sliced
6 heaping tablespoons miso paste (mild, sweet
   white, or red)
1 cup chopped watercress
18 cherry tomatoes, halved
1½ cups diced tofu (optional)
3 scallions, white and tender greens, minced
Daikon or radishes, thinly sliced

EQUIPMENT:
6-quart covered stockpot
2-quart covered saucepan with steamer

Cook noodles in stock pot according to package directions in 3½ quarts water. When noodles are cooked, drain, reserving the water and noodles separately. Briefly steam carrots and mushrooms in saucepan for 3 to 5 minutes. The vegetables should stay firm. Remove vegetable steamer from heat. Add watercress and tomatoes to the steamer and cover. The greens will wilt, and the tomatoes will pucker but won't overcook.

For each person, place 1 heaping tablespoon of miso in individual large soup bowls. Divide the reserved noodle-water among the soup bowls. With a large wooden spoon, mash the miso against the side of each bowl until the paste completely dissolves, yielding a miso broth. Add the noodles, vegetables, and tofu to the bowls; garnish with scallions and radish. **Serves 6.** ●

PENNSYLVANIA DUTCH
CHICKEN-CORN SOUP

INGREDIENTS:
1 broiler or frying chicken, 3 to 4 pounds, cut into quarters, rinsed
3 stalks celery with leaves, coarsely chopped
4 large yellow onions, coarsely chopped
2 medium carrots, peeled and coarsely chopped
3 quarts water
1 teaspoon salt
2 cups fresh corn kernels cut from the cob (or frozen white-corn kernels)
½ cup chopped fresh parsley
½ pound wide egg noodles, broken into small pieces
Salt and freshly ground black pepper to taste
1 red bell pepper, cored, seeded, and chopped, for garnish
3 hard-boiled eggs for garnish (optional)

EQUIPMENT:
8-quart covered stockpot

In stockpot, cover chicken, celery, onions, and carrots with water. Add 1 teaspoon salt. Bring to boil, and boil vigorously 15 minutes, skimming off any scum that accumulates on the surface. Reduce heat, cover, and simmer 2 hours, skimming as necessary.

Remove from heat and refrigerate until cool enough to handle. Remove chicken from liquid; skin, debone, and cut into bite-sized pieces. Return broth to a boil and add corn, parsley, noodles, salt, and pepper. After 5 minutes, add chicken. Reduce heat and simmer 5 more minutes. Garnish servings with slices of hard-boiled egg or chopped red pepper if desired. **Serves 6 to 8.**

TIP: To reduce fat content, cook chicken and refrigerate overnight. Fat will rise to the top and solidify so that it can be easily removed and discarded. Skinning the chicken before making broth will remove more of the fat, but also some of the flavor.

POTATO-PLUS SOUP

INGREDIENTS:
2 quarts water
1 large red potato, unpeeled
1 medium Idaho potato, peeled
1 medium yam, peeled
2 carrots, scrubbed well or peeled
1 large onion, peeled
2 turnips, peeled
2 parsnips, peeled
2 stalks celery, including leaves
1 tablespoon fresh rosemary leaves or dill or 1 teaspoon dried ground cardamom
Salt and freshly ground black pepper to taste
Plain yogurt or sour cream for garnish (optional)
Fresh chopped parsley for garnish

EQUIPMENT:
4½-quart covered Dutch oven or stockpot

Bring water to a boil. Cut all vegetables into small dice; add to boiling water. Add herbs and seasoning to taste; reduce heat and simmer, covered, 4 hours or more, adding water as necessary. Garnish each serving as desired. **Serves 6.** ● ■ ▼

Pennsylvania Dutch Chicken-Corn Soup

New Year's Eve Supper

Italian Seafood Stew or Vegetable Pistou
Italian Bread with Olive Oil and Herbs
Insalata Tricolore
Chocolate Torte or Gingerbread Cake
Iced Winter Fruit
After-dinner Cheeses—Mascarpone and Bleu de Bresse

Iced Winter Fruit and *Gingerbread Cake*

New Year's Eve can be celebrated in many ways. One favorite is a simple, satisfying supper served picnic style, preferably in front of a roaring fire. It can be enjoyed by any number of people, from two to eight or more. Whether you entertain family and friends, or plan a romantic dinner *à deux*, after the rush of Thanksgiving, Hanukkah, and Christmas, it's a treat to relax and partake of this simple yet memorable meal.

All you need for an indoor picnic is a heavy tablecloth on a carpeted floor and a few lounging pillows. If you have picnic baskets, use them to store plates for the meal and extra napkins, to hide the dessert for a surprise presentation, or to store a bag of confetti to toss at midnight. Arrange everything close at hand, so you don't have to keep getting up. Only the *Iced Winter Fruit* needs to remain in the refrigerator/freezer until served.

An all-white decor with touches of gold is a particularly attractive New Year's Eve setting. Above all, keep it simple and uncomplicated . . . the last day of the year shouldn't be spent rushing around so much that you collapse with exhaustion on New Year's Eve. Try a plain white tablecloth and cutlery wrapped in white cloth napkins tied with gold ribbons. For a festive air, tie "bouquets" of white or gold helium balloons with colored paper streamers to the picnic basket handles. And don't forget the noisemakers!

Prepare Ahead:

If you're serving the *Vegetable Pistou* (see p. 41), make it the day before. The *Italian Seafood Stew* (see p. 43) can be done ahead of time up to the addition of shrimp and scallops.

The *Chocolate Torte* (see p. 151) or *Gingerbread Cake* (see p. 150) can also be prepared a day ahead. The *Iced Winter Fruit* (see p. 148) should be prepared no earlier than the morning of the day you will be serving it.

The *Italian Bread* (see p. 138) and *Insalata Tricolore* (see p. 26) without the dressing can be prepared in the morning.

Plan to allow an hour to assemble the meal that evening, then relax and have a Happy New Year.

HOT AND SPICY BLACK BEAN SOUP

You don't have to soak the beans—they become tender during the cooking process. Serve with flour tortillas (see p. 136).

INGREDIENTS:

6 cups water
2 cups dried black beans, rinsed
1 medium onion, finely chopped
1 garlic clove, minced
3 red bell peppers, cored, seeded, and chopped
1 to 2 jalapeño peppers, seeded and diced
¾ cup red wine
½ teaspoon dried thyme
½ teaspoon dried oregano
For the Garnish:
¾ cup plain yogurt or sour cream
1 bunch scallions, white and tender greens, chopped
1½ tablespoons chopped fresh cilantro leaves

EQUIPMENT:
8-quart covered stockpot

Bring water to a boil in stockpot; add beans, onion, and garlic. Reduce heat, cover, and simmer 1½ to 2 hours, adding more water if soup becomes too thick. Add remaining ingredients, except garnish, and cook one more hour. Garnish each serving with a dollop of yogurt or sour cream, chopped scallions, and cilantro. **Serves 6.** ● ▼

TIP: To peel peppers without broiling, use a swivel-bladed potato peeler with a sawing motion to remove most of peel. This isn't necessary but will result in a smoother soup.

WATERCRESS AND SPINACH SOUP

Quick, easy, delicious—a wonderful first-course soup for any meal.

INGREDIENTS:

1 tablespoon unsalted butter or margarine
2 shallots, chopped
2 cups chopped watercress leaves
2 cups chopped spinach leaves
6 cups chicken broth, canned or homemade
4 tablespoons farina (instant Cream of Wheat)
Salt and freshly ground black pepper to taste

EQUIPMENT:

8-inch sauté pan
Food processor or blender
4-quart covered saucepan

Melt butter in sauté pan over medium heat; add shallots and sauté, stirring 3 to 5 minutes. Place in food processor with ⅓ of the watercress and spinach and 1½ cups of the chicken broth. Puree and remove to saucepan. Add remaining watercress, spinach, and chicken broth. Bring to a boil; add farina and stir 2 to 3 minutes. Reduce heat and simmer, partially covered, 10 minutes. Add salt and pepper to taste. **Serves 6.** ● ■

VARIATION: Add 2 teaspoons of curry powder to the shallots after sautéing and cook for 30 seconds. Continue with recipe. Serve with a dollop of yogurt.

Watercress and Spinach Soup

Gazpacho

GAZPACHO

Now an American classic—for picnics, lunches, dinners, even brunch.

INGREDIENTS:
⅓ cup red-wine vinegar
¼ cup olive oil (optional)
½ cup tomato juice
1 to 2 garlic cloves, halved
4 large tomatoes, chopped
4 scallions, white and tender greens, chopped
2 red, green, or yellow bell peppers, or
  combination, cored, seeded, and chopped
1 large cucumber, peeled and chopped
1 small onion, chopped
Salt and freshly ground black pepper to taste
⅓ cup chopped fresh dill or 2 tablespoons
  chopped fresh basil leaves
Toasted croutons, grated carrots, shredded
  endive, chopped arugula or radicchio, for
  garnish

EQUIPMENT:
Small (1-quart) mixing bowl
Food processor or blender

In bowl, whisk together vinegar, oil, and tomato juice. Add garlic and ⅔ of the vegetables to the container of food processor or blender. Process until vegetables are pureed, gradually adding the tomato juice mixture. Pour into a storage container; stir in remaining vegetables, salt, pepper, and dill or basil. Refrigerate. Garnish as desired. **Serves 6.**

▼ ■

Cold Fruit Soup

COLD FRUIT SOUP

Serve this as a first course—or a surprise dessert.

INGREDIENTS:
4 cups water
½ cup dried apricots, diced
¾ cup pitted prunes, diced
1 orange, peeled and sectioned with white
    membrane removed
½ lemon, quartered
1 cinnamon stick
2½ tablespoons cornstarch
2 cups red wine
1 cup sugar
1 (16-ounce) can pitted sour red cherries with
    juice
¾ cup slivered almonds

EQUIPMENT:
4-quart covered saucepan
Small (1-quart) mixing bowl

Bring water to a boil, add apricots, prunes, orange sections, lemon, and cinnamon stick. Remove from heat, cover, and let stand 30 minutes. In bowl, combine cornstarch and ¼ cup of the red wine, stirring until cornstarch is completely dissolved; add to fruit mixture.

Add the rest of the wine, sugar, and cherries with their juice. Bring to a boil over high heat; reduce heat to low and simmer, stirring occasionally, 10 to 12 minutes. (Mixture will thicken slightly.) Remove lemon and cinnamon stick and chill soup thoroughly. Serve cold in individual bowls, garnished with a sprinkling of slivered almonds. **Serves 4 to 6.** ▼ ■

COLD CUCUMBER SOUP

INGREDIENTS:

2 medium potatoes, peeled and diced
4 cups chicken broth, canned or homemade
3 large cucumbers, peeled, seeded, and coarsely
    grated
4 to 6 scallions, white and tender greens, finely
    chopped
2 tablespoons chopped fresh dill, plus more for
    garnish
½ cup plain yogurt or sour cream
Salt and freshly ground black pepper to taste

EQUIPMENT:

4-quart covered saucepan
Food processor or blender

Place potatoes and broth in saucepan; bring to a boil and cook, covered, over medium-high heat 15 minutes or until tender. Remove from heat and puree potatoes and liquid briefly in food processor or blender. This step may need to be done in two batches. Return mixture to saucepan. Add cucumbers, scallions, and 2 tablespoons dill to saucepan. Bring to a boil; reduce heat and simmer 15 minutes. Remove from heat and refrigerate. When cooled—but not cold—add yogurt or sour cream. Mix well and return to refrigerator to chill thoroughly. Salt and pepper to taste just before serving. Sprinkle each serving with chopped dill. **Serves 6.** ● ■

VEGETABLE PISTOU

In French *pistou* translates as "dried basil," but it's really more like the French version of Italian pesto—a blend of olive oil, basil, and garlic—and is a frequent addition to soups.

INGREDIENTS:

4 quarts water or vegetable broth (see p. 33)
4 medium carrots, peeled and cut in 2-inch
    lengths
2 large leeks, white and tender greens, chopped
2 medium zucchini, cut in ¾-inch rounds
6 small new potatoes, halved or quartered
    depending on size
½ pound fresh green beans
Salt and freshly ground black pepper to taste
4 garlic cloves, peeled
12 to 16 fresh basil leaves
3 tomatoes, peeled and quartered
½ cup olive oil
1 cup grated Gruyère cheese, or grated
    Parmesan cheese

EQUIPMENT:

8-quart covered stockpot
Food processor or blender

To boiling water, add carrots, leeks, zucchini, potatoes, and half of the green beans. Return to boil, reduce heat, and simmer gently 1½ hours. Add salt and pepper to taste. Puree the garlic, basil, tomatoes, and olive oil in blender or food processor. Add puree to soup and cook 8 to 10 minutes. Add remaining green beans and cook 6 more minutes. Just before serving, top each bowl of soup with cheese. **Serves 6.** ▼

TIP: After vegetables have cooked 30 minutes, transfer several pieces of each vegetable to food processor or blender. Puree and return to stockpot. This will intensify the vegetable broth and trim cooking time by about 30 minutes. Cook for an additional half hour before adding pistou—the pureed garlic, basil, tomatoes, and olive oil.

BEEF STEW

INGREDIENTS:

2½ to 3 pounds lean beef chuck or round, cut into 1½-inch cubes
2 to 3 medium-sized onions, quartered
6 tablespoons vegetable or olive oil
¼ cup flour
2 teaspoons freshly ground black pepper
1 cup red wine
3 to 4 carrots, cut into 1-inch lengths
1 white turnip or parsnip, peeled and coarsely chopped
1 bay leaf
2 cloves garlic, coarsely chopped
½ teaspoon dried thyme
2 (10½-ounce) cans beef broth
4 to 5 medium potatoes, peeled and quartered
2 stalks celery with leaves, cut into 1-inch lengths
1 (28-ounce) can Italian plum tomatoes, drained and juice reserved

EQUIPMENT:

10-inch skillet
6-quart covered Dutch oven or casserole

TIP: See Vigorous Veal Stew TIP, p. 43.

VARIATIONS:

Be creative with the different vegetables that you add to the stew! Try:

● Leeks, chopped, or chopped shallots in place of onions

● Yams, peeled and cubed, in place of white potatoes

● Brussels sprouts, trimmed, added 15 minutes before stew is done

● Okra, both ends trimmed, added 10 to 15 minutes before stew is done

● Broccoli or cauliflower florets, added 10 minutes before stew is done

● Mushrooms, quartered if large, added 10 minutes before stew is done

● Fresh corn kernels, added 10 minutes before stew is done; frozen corn kernels, added 5 minutes before stew is done

● Bell-pepper strips, added 5 minutes before stew is done

● Green cabbage, cored and shredded, added 5 minutes before stew is done

● Green beans, cut in 2-inch pieces, added 10 minutes before stew is done.

Dry meat well with paper towels. Add onions and half the oil to skillet. Cook, stirring frequently, over medium heat, until onions soften. Remove onion with slotted spoon and reserve. Add enough meat to cover the bottom of the skillet without overcrowding and having cubes touch; brown cubes on at least two sides. Remove browned meat to Dutch oven or casserole; continue to brown the rest of the cubes, adding remaining oil as necessary.

Preheat oven to 350°. Sprinkle meat with flour and pepper, tossing until flour disappears. Pour off any fat remaining in skillet. Return skillet to medium heat, add half the wine and stir with a wooden spoon to scrape the brown bits from the bottom of the pan. Pour this mixture over meat, add remaining wine, and stir. Add reserved onion, carrots, turnip or parsnip, bay leaf, garlic, thyme, and beef broth (it will provide all the salt you'll need). Stir again, then bring to a simmer. Cover and place in oven. After 15 minutes, reduce heat to 300° and cook 1½ hours.

Add potatoes, celery, and tomatoes. (If tomatoes are whole, break them up by hand, reserving juice.) If stew needs more liquid, add reserved juice from tomatoes. Cook 20 to 25 more minutes, or until potatoes are tender. Remove bay leaf before serving. **Serves 8.**

Italian Seafood Stew

VIGOROUS VEAL STEW

Balsamic vinegar gives this dish its distinctive tang.

INGREDIENTS:
3 tablespoons olive oil
3 pounds veal shoulder or rump, trimmed of all
   fat and cubed
¾ cup finely chopped onion
1 or more cups beef broth, canned or homemade
4 tablespoons balsamic vinegar
1½ cups chopped fresh or canned Italian plum
   tomatoes
¾ teaspoon dried rosemary
Salt and freshly ground black pepper to taste

EQUIPMENT:
4½-quart covered Dutch oven

Heat 2 tablespoons of the oil over high heat. Dry meat with paper towels. Add veal cubes a few at a time and brown on all sides. As the meat is browned, remove and set aside. Add remaining oil, lower heat, and sauté onion until golden, about 3 minutes. Stir in ⅔ cup of the broth, 3 tablespoons of the vinegar, ½ cup of the tomatoes, and ½ teaspoon of the dried rosemary. Mix well.

Return browned veal to the pan, cover, and simmer over low heat 1 to 1½ hours, or until meat is tender. You may need to add more broth. Just before serving, stir in remaining vinegar, tomatoes, rosemary, and more broth if necessary. Season with salt and pepper, then simmer 10 minutes. **Serves 6.**

TIP: When removing meat from a pan, use tongs insteak of a fork to avoid losing juices.

ITALIAN SEAFOOD STEW

INGREDIENTS:
½ cup olive oil
3 garlic cloves, 2 cloves finely minced and 1 clove
   halved
1 medium onion, coarsely chopped
½ pound calamari (squid), boned, cleaned (have
   your fish market do this), and cut into rings
¾ cup dry white wine
3 cups tomato puree
1 small bunch fresh Italian flat-leaf parsley,
   chopped
¼ cup water
1½ pounds cod fillet or other firm white fish
Dash of Tabasco sauce
½ pound medium shrimp, shelled and deveined
½ pound whole bay scallops or sea scallops
4 slices Italian bread
¼ cup coarsely chopped fresh Italian parsley

EQUIPMENT:
6-quart covered stockpot

Put oil in stockpot over medium heat and lightly sauté minced garlic and onion, about 5 minutes. Add squid, wine, 1 cup of the tomato puree, parsley, and water; cover and cook over low heat 30 minutes or until squid is tender.

Add remaining 2 cups tomato puree, white fish, and Tabasco; cover and simmer 10 minutes or until fish is tender. Add shrimp and scallops and cook until shrimp turns pink, 5 to 7 minutes, but no more. If necessary, add a little water, but the stew should be thick.

Toast the Italian bread and rub each slice with the cut garlic clove. Place a slice of bread in each soup bowl and ladle stew over it. Garnish with chopped parsley. **Serves 4 to 6.**

TIP: You can use the shrimp shells to make a broth. Add shells to 2½ cups water. Bring to a boil and simmer for about 15 to 20 minutes until liquid has reduced to 2 cups. Strain and use to replace the water and wine, refrigerate or freeze the remainder for use in fish or vegetable soups.

POULTRY

Poultry is served the world over; its versatility, and in America its relatively low cost make it a staple entree. Since you, too, probably serve it often, we've included a variety of international flavors in our chicken recipes—from Mexico, Asia, France, India, and Scandinavia—to broaden your family's horizons.

By removing the skin before or after cooking you can cut down the fat content considerably. About half of the fat found in poultry is in its skin. The skin does protect the meat from drying out, however, which is why some cooks prefer to remove the skin *after* cooking.

To cook chicken without using additional fats, try roasting, grilling, broiling, or poaching. Chicken poached in water seasoned with herbs, vegetables, or wine is a delicious meal. To reduce the fat in chicken sauté recipes, poach the chicken first. Sauté all ingredients except the chicken (you'll need significantly less butter or oil than the recipe calls for). Then combine with poached chicken, toss well, and serve.

CLEANING POULTRY

To protect yourself against salmonella, always thoroughly rinse poultry before cooking. Hold under cold running water. If you're using a whole bird, rinse the cavity as well. The knives and surface you use to cut raw poultry should be thoroughly washed with soap and hot water afterward. And so should your hands.

ORANGE CHICKEN

Serve this on a bed of fresh blanched or steamed spinach, drizzled
with sauce from the chicken. It's a quick, easy, and elegant meal.

INGREDIENTS:
½ cup dry white wine
¼ cup fresh orange juice
2 teaspoons Dijon-style or prepared brown
  mustard
1 orange, any variety, peeled, seeded, and sliced
½ red onion, thinly sliced
2 whole chicken breasts, rinsed, skinned, boned,
  and cut in strips
1 sprig fresh rosemary
Salt and freshly ground black pepper to taste

EQUIPMENT:
10-inch sauté pan

Combine wine, orange juice, and mustard in sauté pan over medium-high heat and stir until well blended. Add orange slices, onion, chicken, and rosemary and simmer uncovered, stirring occasionally, 5 to 8 minutes or until chicken is cooked through. Season to taste. **Serves 4.** ● ■

Orange Chicken

CHICKEN WITH LEMON AND HERBS

INGREDIENTS:
Broiler-fryer, 3½ to 4 pounds, rinsed, skinned, and cut in serving-size pieces
3 tablespoons butter or margarine
4 lemon slices
¾ teaspoons dried thyme
½ teaspoon dried sage
Salt and freshly ground black pepper to taste
3 tablespoons all-purpose flour
1 cup light cream
½ cup sour cream
¼ cup water

EQUIPMENT:
10-inch sauté pan
Casserole or ovenproof serving dish

In sauté pan, sauté chicken in butter over medium heat, turning frequently until pieces are lightly browned. Add lemon slices, sprinkle chicken with thyme, sage, salt, and pepper, and cover. Lower heat and simmer 30 minutes.

Remove chicken to ovenproof serving dish and keep warm. Add flour to juices in the sauté pan and stir until smooth. Add remaining ingredients and a pinch of salt, if desired, and cook over low heat stirring constantly until mixture thickens. Discard lemon slices, pour sauce over chicken, and serve. **Serves 4.**

TIP: Put casserole in a warm (300°) oven when you begin to cook chicken, then lower oven to low when chicken is placed in it. It will stay warm nicely.

CURRIED CHICKEN-BROCCOLI CASSEROLE

Serve over rice to catch the sauce and make a complete meal.

INGREDIENTS:
1½ pounds, 1 large bunch, fresh broccoli, broken into six to eight stalks
2 tablespoons butter or margarine
2 tablespoons vegetable oil
3 whole chicken breasts, rinsed, skinned, and cut in half
Salt and freshly ground black pepper to taste.
1 recipe Béchamel Sauce (see p. 124)
3 tablespoons curry powder
3 tablespoons light cream
Generous squeeze fresh lemon (optional)

EQUIPMENT:
2-quart covered saucepan with steamer
3-quart covered casserole
1-quart saucepan

Cook broccoli for 5 minutes in steamer. Preheat oven to 350°. In casserole over medium-high heat, cook butter and oil until it foams. Place chicken breasts in one layer and brown 2 to 3 minutes on each side. Remove chicken; drain off all fat and wipe pan with a paper towel.

In small saucepan, prepare Béchamel Sauce—or reheat previously prepared sauce, adding curry powder during last few minutes of cooking. Add cream one tablespoon at a time, blending well, and a squeeze of lemon. Put broccoli in casserole, add chicken and sprinkle with salt and pepper. Pour sauce over chicken and broccoli and bake covered 15 minutes. Remove lid and bake 10 to 15 more minutes until chicken is cooked through. Serve over rice. **Serves 6.**

TIP: To reduce fat, poach the chicken instead of browning it in butter and oil.

BAKED TARRAGON CHICKEN

INGREDIENTS:
2 whole chicken breasts, rinsed and cut in half
1 tablespoon plus 1 teaspoon dried tarragon
Salt and freshly ground black or white pepper to
taste

EQUIPMENT:
Shallow roasting pan with rack

Preheat oven to 375°. Sprinkle each chicken
breast with 1 teaspoon of tarragon, salt, and pepper.
Place chicken on rack in a shallow roasting pan and
bake 25 to 30 minutes, or until skin is golden brown
and juices run clear when breast is pricked with a
fork. **Serves 4.**

VARIATION: To reduce fat and cholesterol, remove skin from chicken breasts. Blend tarragon
with 2 to 3 tablespoons vegetable or olive oil and
baste both sides of each chicken piece. Baste peri-
odically so that chicken won't dry out. ● ■

Herbed Chicken

HERBED CHICKEN

INGREDIENTS:
2 whole chicken breasts, rinsed, skinned, boned,
and cut in half
3 tablespoons all-purpose flour
¼ teaspoon dried thyme
Several grinds of a pepper mill containing mixed
peppercorns or pepper
2 tablespoons butter or margarine
¼ cup chicken broth, canned or homemade
1 teaspoon tomato paste
1 garlic clove, mashed
Salt to taste
1 tablespoon chopped fresh chives or tender
green onion tops

EQUIPMENT:
Pie plate
10-inch sauté pan
Small bowl or 2–cup measuring cup

VARIATION: Add extra flavor by adding 5 or 6
sliced mushrooms to the broth mixture and cooking
for 3 minutes, stirring once.

Using a "hit and slide" motion to avoid tearing
meat, flatten chicken breasts with meat pounder or
bottom of a small, heavy skillet. Mix flour, thyme,
and pepper in pie plate. Dip chicken in flour mixture to coat. Preheat sauté pan over high heat. Add
butter and rotate pan to coat entire cooking surface.
Do not let butter brown. Add chicken, pressing
down on each piece with a spatula to sear underside.
Cook over high heat 1 minute; turn and cook other
side in the same way 1 minute. Lower heat and cook
6 to 8 minutes or until chicken is cooked through.
Remove chicken to a warm platter.

Mix together broth, tomato paste, garlic, and
salt. Add broth mixture to pan; use wooden spoon
to stir and scrape bits of chicken from pan bottom.
Cook 2 minutes, stirring gently. Pour over chicken;
top with chives and serve. **Serves 4.**

TIP: Combine 1 tablespoon each black and white
peppercorns with 1 teaspoon each whole coriander and allspice to make mixed peppercorns. Use
in poultry and fish dishes.

Japanese Chicken, Carrots, and Parsnips

JAPANESE CHICKEN, CARROTS, AND PARSNIPS

Try this healthy, delicately flavored dish served over rice with a small spinach salad (see p. 26) on the side.

INGREDIENTS:

2 whole chicken breasts, rinsed, skinned, boned, and cut into bite-sized pieces

¼ cup soy sauce

12 baby carrots, scrubbed and quartered

6 young parsnips, peeled and sliced in thin rounds

1 tablespoon grated fresh ginger

2 teaspoons vegetable or peanut oil

1 tablespoon white or rice vinegar

Pinch of sugar

2 to 3 scallions for garnish, white and tender greens, sliced lengthwise

EQUIPMENT:

Glass pie plate

3-quart covered double boiler

Small bowl or 2-cup measuring cup

Place chicken and soy sauce in pie plate, mix to coat and marinate 15 minutes, stirring occasionally. Put chicken with sauce in top of double boiler. Add carrots and parsnips. Cover with ginger. Mix together oil, vinegar, and sugar; drizzle over chicken and vegetables. Cover and cook 10 to 15 minutes over boiling water. Garnish with fresh scallions. **Serves 6.** ● ■

Mexican Chicken with Tomato-Raisin Sauce

MEXICAN CHICKEN
WITH TOMATO-RAISIN SAUCE

This Tomato-Raisin Sauce is also terrific served over shredded left-over roast chicken or turkey on a bed of white rice.

INGREDIENTS:

⅓ pound hot or sweet Italian sausage, coarsely chopped
1 tablespoon olive oil
1 small onion, finely chopped
¼ cup raisins
Dash of cayenne pepper or chili powder
1 medium tomato, coarsely chopped
1 cup canned crushed tomatoes in puree
1 tablespoon dry red wine
¼ cup slivered almonds
2 whole chicken breasts, rinsed, skinned, boned, and cut in half
2 tablespoons olive oil
1 heaping tablespoon minced garlic
Salt and freshly ground black pepper to taste

EQUIPMENT:

2 10-inch sauté pans
Cookie sheet

In one sauté pan, cook sausage until it's cooked through but not brown or crispy, then drain on paper towels. In the other sauté pan, over medium heat, add oil and cook onion, raisins, and pepper 5 minutes. Add fresh and canned tomato, wine, and sausage. Bring to a boil, reduce heat, and simmer 50 minutes.

Preheat oven to 400°. Spread almonds on a cookie sheet and toast them in oven for 1 minute. (Watch them carefully so that they don't brown too much.) Remove from oven and set aside. Five minutes before the sauce is finished simmering, add toasted almonds and mix well.

Flatten chicken breasts slightly with a meat pounder (see *Herbed Chicken*, p. 47). Heat oil in sauté pan over medium heat. Add garlic and sauté 1 minute. Add chicken breasts and cook through, turning them frequently so that they don't stick—about 8 to 10 minutes total. Transfer chicken to a serving platter and top each breast generously with Tomato-Raisin Sauce. **Serves 4.**

TURKEY PICCATA

This variation of veal piccata is just as good and costs less than half as much!

INGREDIENTS:

8 skinless, boneless turkey-breast cutlets, about 3 ounces each, rinsed
⅓ cup flour
Salt and freshly ground black pepper to taste
8 tablespoons (1 stick) unsalted butter
¼ cup fresh lemon juice
8 paper-thin lemon slices
Chopped parsley for garnish

EQUIPMENT:

Pie plate
10-inch sauté pan

Place each turkey cutlet between two pieces of wax paper and, being careful not to break the flesh, pound gently with a meat pounder to flatten. Combine flour, salt, and pepper in pie plate. Dip both sides of each cutlet in flour mixture. Melt 2 tablespoons butter in skillet over medium heat and sauté 4 of the cutlets briefly until golden brown, about 1 minute to a side; remove from pan. Melt 4 more tablespoons butter and repeat the process with remaining cutlets.

Add remaining 2 tablespoons of butter and lemon juice to sauté pan and cook about 1 minute, stirring constantly to scrape up the brown bits stuck to the pan. Pour sauce over cutlets, garnish each with a lemon slice, and sprinkle with chopped parsley. Serve immediately. **Serves 4 to 6.**

SPICY OVEN-"FRIED" CHICKEN

INGREDIENTS:

1 cup plain dried bread crumbs
2 tablespoons dried coriander
1 tablespoon dried cumin
1 teaspoon onion powder
1 teaspoon garlic powder
1 teaspoon cinnamon
Dash of cayenne pepper or freshly ground black pepper to taste
3 egg whites
6 chicken legs, rinsed and trimmed of fat
6 chicken thighs, rinsed and trimmed of fat

EQUIPMENT:

Deep roasting pan with rack
Medium (2½-quart) mixing bowl
Pie plate

Preheat oven to 375°. Line roasting pan with aluminum foil. In pie plate, combine first seven ingredients. Beat egg whites in bowl and set aside. Dip each piece of chicken in beaten egg white, let excess egg white drip off, then dredge in seasoned bread crumbs. Arrange breaded chicken in roasting pan and bake 35 to 40 minutes, moving pieces once or twice during baking to prevent sticking. **Serves 6.**

TIP: To minimize sticking and avoid the need for turning, put chicken on a rack in the pan.

SAUTÉ WITH LESS FAT: Many people don't sauté correctly. They use too little heat and too much fat. Keep the heat high, and don't overcrowd the pan, or the temperature will be lowered so much that the food will steam rather than sauté. The pan should be very hot before the oil is put in. If it's hot enough, the food is less likely to stick, and you'll need less oil.

SCANDINAVIAN CHICKEN LOAF

A healthful, tasty alternative to meat loaf. Cold, it makes a wonderful sandwich filler. It can also be sliced and served as a country pâté.

INGREDIENTS:

2 pounds ground chicken or turkey
3 tablespoons chopped onion
1 small, tart apple, unpeeled, cored, and finely chopped
2 tablespoons finely chopped red bell pepper
3 heaping tablespoons golden raisins
1 egg or 2 egg whites, lightly beaten
2 tablespoons white-wine Worcestershire sauce
¼ teaspoon allspice
Salt and freshly ground white pepper to taste
¼ cup apple juice or cider

EQUIPMENT:

Large (4-quart) mixing bowl
Loaf pan

Preheat oven to 350°. Combine all ingredients except apple juice in bowl and mix well. Place in loaf pan, cover with aluminum foil, and bake 25 minutes. Remove foil, pour apple juice over loaf, and bake 25 more minutes. **Serves 6.** ● ■

Scandinavian Chicken Loaf

Poached Chicken with Vegetables

POACHED CHICKEN WITH VEGETABLES

INGREDIENTS:

6 young carrots, scrubbed and quartered
1 onion, sliced
4 celery stalks, chopped
3 cups chicken broth, canned or homemade
1 frying or broiling chicken, about 3½ pounds, rinsed, cut into pieces, skin removed
2 cups dry white wine
2 tablespoons fresh tarragon leaves or 2 teaspoons dried tarragon
1 bay leaf
1 pound asparagus, cut into bite-sized pieces
3 to 4 cups *cooked* rice or couscous

EQUIPMENT:

6-quart covered Dutch oven

In Dutch oven, simmer carrots, onion, and celery in 2 cups chicken broth for 10 minutes. Add chicken, remaining broth, herbs, and wine, cover and simmer 25 minutes or until chicken is cooked through. Add asparagus 5 to 10 minutes before dish is completely cooked. Tip pan to skim off fat. Remove chicken pieces and vegetables: arrange them over rice on individual serving plates and pour some of broth over each serving. **Serves 4 to 6.** ● ■

TIP: For a richer broth, but one with a little more fat, cook the chicken with the skin on; remove skin before serving.

Country Roasted Chicken and *Herb Stuffing*

COUNTRY
ROASTED CHICKEN

INGREDIENTS:

1 roasting chicken, about 3 pounds, rinsed inside and out
Salt, freshly ground black pepper, and paprika
2 medium onions, quartered
6 garlic cloves, halved
2 lemons, quartered
6 small sprigs fresh rosemary
¼ cup or more apple-cider vinegar

EQUIPMENT:

Shallow roasting pan with rack

Preheat oven to 350°. Remove giblets and discard; season chicken cavity with salt, pepper, and paprika. Then stuff with onion, garlic, 6 lemon wedges, and 4 rosemary sprigs. Squeeze the juice from the 2 remaining lemon wedges over skin, then sprinkle with rosemary leaves, pepper, and paprika. Put squeezed lemon wedges inside cavity, tuck flap of skin at neck under bird, and place it breast-side up on rack in pan. Cover loosely with aluminum foil and bake on middle rack of oven 15 to 20 minutes. Remove aluminum foil, add cider vinegar to pan, and roast uncovered 1 to 1½ hours more or until done, basting with juices every 20 minutes. (You may need to add more vinegar if the pan becomes dry.) Before serving, discard onion, garlic, lemon, and herbs. **Serves 4 to 6.**

HERB STUFFING

This garden-green stuffing is excellent with chicken, Cornish game hens, or baked fish.

INGREDIENTS:

4 tablespoons butter or margarine
4 shallots, minced
2 stalks tender young celery with leaves, cut into 2-inch lengths
1 cup fresh parsley
½ cup watercress
⅔ cup crumbled, crustless bread
4 fresh basil leaves
1 egg
½ cup fresh bread crumbs
6 water chestnuts, chopped
Salt and freshly ground black pepper to taste

EQUIPMENT:

8-inch sauté pan
Food processor or blender
Large (4-quart) mixing bowl

Melt butter in sauté pan over medium heat and sauté shallots 2 to 3 minutes. Remove from heat, cool slightly, and put in container of food processor. Add celery, parsley, watercress, bread, basil, and egg and puree.

Place bread crumbs and water chestnuts in bowl. Add puree and blend well with a fork. Season with salt and pepper. Bake at 350° for 30 minutes if serving separately. **Yield: about 2½ cups.**

WILD-RICE STUFFING A L'ORANGE

Perfect for stuffing Cornish game hens or a roasting chicken.

INGREDIENTS:
Giblets and necks of game hens or chicken, rinsed
4 cups water
Pinch of salt
1 cup wild rice
4 tablespoons butter or margarine
3 shallots, minced
1 tablespoon finely chopped green bell pepper
1 tablespoon finely grated orange rind
Salt and freshly ground pepper to taste

EQUIPMENT:
2½-quart covered saucepan
10-inch sauté pan

Bring salted water to a boil in saucepan. Add giblets and necks, reduce heat, and simmer about 20 minutes. Remove giblets, chop, and reserve; discard necks. Raise heat to high, bring stock to a rolling boil, and add wild rice. Lower heat immediately, cover, and simmer, stirring occasionally, 30 minutes, or until rice is almost tender and most of the stock is absorbed.

Melt butter in sauté pan and sauté shallots and green pepper 3 minutes. Remove from heat. Add chopped giblets, grated orange rind, drained rice, salt, and pepper to the shallots and green pepper in the pan, mixing well. **Yield: about 3 cups.**

Wild Rice Stuffing a l'Orange

OYSTER STUFFING

This oyster stuffing recipe makes enough for a 15- to 20-pound turkey. Bake any extra stuffing at 350° in a greased baking dish for 30 minutes.

INGREDIENTS:
1 pint shucked oysters with their liquor
6 tablespoons butter
2 cups finely chopped onions
1½ cups finely chopped celery, including a few celery leaves
1 garlic clove, minced
½ teaspoon dried thyme
5 cups fresh bread crumbs
1 cup finely chopped fresh Italian flat-leaf parsley
Salt and freshly ground black pepper to taste
2 eggs, lightly beaten

EQUIPMENT:
10-inch sauté pan

Drain oysters, reserving the liquor, and cut each in half. Melt butter in sauté pan over medium heat; add onion, celery, garlic, and thyme. Cook 5 minutes, stirring constantly. Add oyster liquor and cook 8 to 10 minutes, stirring occasionally. Add oysters and cook, stirring, about 10 *seconds*. Remove from heat and allow to cool to room temperature, then add bread crumbs, parsley, salt, pepper, and eggs and blend well. Unless you're going to stuff and roast the bird immediately, refrigerate stuffing until ready to use. **Yield: about 8 cups.**

ROAST TURKEY

Turkey is one of the leanest types of poultry. The exception to that is the self-basting variety, which is injected with butter or corn, soybean, or coconut oil.

INGREDIENTS:
1 fresh turkey, about 15 pounds
8 cups stuffing of your choice (see p.52-53)
Unsalted butter
For the gravy:
3½ cups liquid, either giblet stock, canned
   chicken stock, or water
¼ cup flour
½ cup water
Salt and freshly ground black pepper to taste

EQUIPMENT:
Deep roasting pan with rack
2-quart saucepan
Small bowl or 2-cup measuring cup

COOKING TIMES: Allow 15 to 20 minutes per pound; for a turkey over 16 pounds, allow 13 to 15 minutes per pound. Add 5 minutes per pound for a stuffed turkey. For more accurate timing, insert a thermometer in center of inner thigh and cook until it reaches 185°. Prick the skin of the thigh to see if the juice runs clear.

TIP: Giblet stock can be made by simmering giblets with 1 whole onion and 1 scrubbed carrot in 4 cups water for 1 hour; discard vegetables and giblets, and strain.

Preheat oven to 450°. Remove giblets and reserve if making stock (see below). Rinse turkey well inside and out. Pat dry and put about 6 cups stuffing into turkey cavity and another 2 cups stuffing in neck area. Fill the cavity and neck only ¾ full to allow room for the stuffing to swell as it cooks. *Note:* Never stuff a turkey until you're ready to roast it; a stuffed turkey is a breeding ground for bacteria. Close cavity opening with small skewers and a crisscrossed string. Secure neck flap under turkey. Fasten legs close to body with string.

Rub skin with butter and place bird, breast side up, on rack in uncovered roasting pan. Reduce oven heat to 325°, and roast according to directions below. After 30 minutes begin basting turkey with pan drippings, chicken broth, or butter, at least once every hour. Let turkey stand a minimum of 15 minutes before carving.

To make gravy, pour off and strain pan juices into a saucepan. Remove fat by tipping pan and skimming off fat with a spoon. Add giblet stock, canned chicken stock, or water until you have about 3½ cups. Heat to a simmer. In small bowl, stir flour into ¼ cup water; add to saucepan a little at a time, stirring constantly with a whisk until well blended. Heat to a boil and simmer 5 minutes. Salt and pepper to taste. **Serves 8 to 10.**

CORNISH GAME HENS EN CASSEROLE

INGREDIENTS:
4 Cornish game hens, about 1 pound each, rinsed
Salt and freshly ground black pepper to taste
2 tablespoons soy, corn, or vegetable oil
8 small white onions, peeled
1 pound fresh mushrooms, trimmed and thinly
   sliced
1 bay leaf
½ teaspoon dried thyme
4 medium-sized carrots, peeled and cut into ½-
   inch rounds
½ cup dry white wine
½ cup chicken broth, canned or homemade
3 tablespoons finely chopped fresh parsley

EQUIPMENT:
6-quart Dutch oven or covered casserole

Sprinkle hens with salt and pepper inside and out; truss with string. Heat oil in Dutch oven over medium-high heat and brown hens all over. Add onions. Continue browning hens and onions, turning frequently, about 5 to 7 minutes. Add mushrooms, bay leaf, and thyme, stir to blend, cover and cook 5 minutes.

Add carrots, wine, and broth, bring to a boil, then cover, reduce heat, and simmer 25 to 30 minutes. Remove bay leaf and sprinkle with parsley before serving. **Serves 4.**

FRESH CRANBERRY-ORANGE RELISH

INGREDIENTS:

12 ounces fresh cranberries, rinsed and picked
    over to remove stems
1 medium seedless orange, cut into eighths, do
    not peel
½ to ¾ cup sugar
½ teaspoon chopped fresh ginger (optional)

EQUIPMENT:

Food processor or blender
Refrigerator storage container

Put half the cranberries and half of the orange sections into the container of a food processor; process until mixture is coarsely chopped with no whole berries remaining. Transfer to a storage container and process the remaining cranberries and orange sections. Combine the two mixtures and stir in sugar to taste. Refrigerate, ideally for several days before serving, to allow flavors to blend. **Yield: about 2½ cups.**

Fresh Cranberry-Orange Relish

ASIAN CHICKEN

This recipe combines traditional Japanese, Chinese, and Indian
ingredients to make a unique Asian dish.

INGREDIENTS:

2 cups all-purpose flour
3 tablespoons curry powder
Whites of 3 eggs, lightly beaten
3 whole chicken breasts, rinsed, skinned, boned,
    and cut in half
¾ cup soy sauce
¾ cup Japanese Mirin cooking wine or ¾ cup
    white wine with 3 tablespoons sugar added
Juice of 1½ lemons
1½ teaspoons light sesame oil
1½ teaspoons Chinese five-spice powder
3 tablespoons peanut or vegetable oil

EQUIPMENT:

Pie plate
Small bowl or 2-cup measuring cup
10-inch sauté pan
9 × 13-inch rectangular baking dish

Preheat oven to 350°. In pie plate, combine flour and curry powder. Dip each chicken breast in beaten egg white, allow the excess to drip off, then dredge both sides in flour-curry mixture; tap gently to shake off excess and set aside.

Combine half the soy sauce with wine, lemon juice, sesame oil, and Chinese five-spice powder. Heat peanut or vegetable oil in pan over medium-high heat about 45 seconds. Sauté chicken in oil until golden brown, about 3 minutes to a side, then place in baking dish. Pour remaining soy sauce into pan (it will smoke a bit) and let it thicken (about 10 seconds), turn off heat and add sauce mixture. Stir well, then pour over chicken and bake 12 minutes. Serve with white or brown rice. **Serves 6.**

TIPS: This is a great make-ahead dish. Prepare as instructed up to baking step, then refrigerate. Allow chicken to return to room temperature, then bake 15 to 17 minutes or until cooked through.

Chinese five-spice powder is sold in most Oriental markets and some supermarkets.

Chicken with Lemon-Mustard Sauce

CHICKEN WITH LEMON-MUSTARD SAUCE

INGREDIENTS:
3 whole chicken breasts, rinsed, skinned, boned,
    and cut in half
Salt and freshly ground black or white pepper to
    taste
1½ cups light cream
4 teaspoons coarse-grained "country" or
    "Parisian"-style mustard
2 tablespoons lemon marmalade
⅛ teaspoon cayenne
2 tablespoons butter or margarine
1 tablespoon vegetable oil
1 tablespoon finely minced fresh chives, Italian
    flat-leaf parsley, or sliced green tops of scallions
    for garnish

EQUIPMENT:
Small (1-quart) mixing bowl
10-inch sauté pan

    Season chicken with salt and pepper. In bowl,
whisk together cream, mustard, marmalade, and
cayenne. Melt butter and oil in sauté pan and sauté
chicken over medium-high heat for 30 seconds on
each side. You may have to do this in two batches.
Reduce heat and add cream mixture. Cook over
medium heat, gently simmering, until sauce is thick
enough to coat the back of a spoon and chicken is
cooked through— approximately 10 minutes. Sprinkle with chives, parsley, or scallions before serving.
Serves 6.

FORMAL DINNER FOR EIGHT

Herbed Olives
New Potatoes with Dill
Assorted Cheeses and Crackers
Cold Cucumber Soup
Cornish Game Hens en Casserole
Double-Wild Rice
Arugula, Grapefruit, and Goat Cheese Salad
Peach Tart
Coffee and Tea

There are few more pleasant social occasions than a dinner party in the home of a friend. But for the host who also happens to be the chef, the prospect can be somewhat daunting. Organizing a formal dinner for eight doesn't have to be a harrowing experience, however. You can relax and enjoy yourself, and your guests will, too, provided you follow the three "Ps" of entertaining—Planning, Practice, and Preparation.

PLANNING

Set the date and time of your party at least three weeks in advance. Make up your invitation list, and either mail out invitations or contact your guests in person or by phone. This is also the time you would ordinarily plan your menu. (Assuming you use the menu we have provided, you're already one step ahead of the game!)

While you're at the planning stage, decide on the seating arrangements for your dinner. Do you have a dining room or dining area with a table large enough to accommodate eight people? If so, you'll no doubt want to use it. But if not, you might consider setting up two card tables. Is space at a premium? Then serve buffet style, and provide a tray table for each person. Depending on your choice, make sure you have the proper linens—a large cloth for the dining table, smaller cloths for card tables, attractive place mats for tray tables, matching or contrasting napkins—and if they need laundering, do them or send them out now.

This is also the time to make up a list of what else you'll need to accomplish in the weeks preceding your party. Since you're the only person who knows your own schedule, only you can decide what should be done when, but try not to leave everything until the last minute.

Is your best china and crystal packed away? Allow time to take it out and wash it if necessary. Does the silver need polishing? Factor that into your calculations. How far in advance can you do whatever housecleaning is necessary so that it will *stay* clean for your party? Will you need to purchase liquor, wine, or other beverages? What about mixers? Ice? Flowers? Write everything down, and check off each item as you take care of it.

Last but not least, go over the recipes for the dishes on the menu. Make a separate list of all the ingredients you will have to buy, remembering to *increase the quantity* of ingredients when necessary to make eight servings.

PRACTICE

As the old saying goes, "Practice makes perfect." So whether you go with the menu provided here or make up one of your own, it's a good idea in the weeks preceding the party to do a trial run of any dishes you have never cooked before. (Your family will be more than happy to act as guinea pigs!) You'll not only feel more confident about preparing the meal for your guests, but you'll also find out if any of the recipe ingredients are hard to find or perhaps not available at all, giving you plenty of time to make any substitutions that may be necessary.

PREPARATION

If you follow the suggestions offered above, you should have no trouble getting organized. And once the logistical headaches are out of the way, you'll be able to devote your attention to the fun part—actually preparing the food.

Since you probably don't want to spend the entire day of your party chained to the stove, the recipes on our menu have been specifically selected so you can do a lot of the preparation in advance. We've even made up a schedule suggesting what can be done when, so you can plan to shop accordingly.

One or Two Weeks Before the Party:

- Make the pastry crust for the *Peach Tart* and freeze. On the morning of your party, thaw the crust and proceed with the recipe. (See recipe, p. 160.)
- Make *Herbed Olives* and store in the refrigerator. The longer they marinate, the better they are. (See recipe, p. 14.)

Two Days Before The Party:

- Purchase assorted cheeses; crackers may be bought at any time.
- Boil the potatoes for *New Potatoes with Dill* and refrigerate; add the topping and garnish right before serving. (See recipe, p. 17.)
- Make *Cold Cucumber Soup* and refrigerate; season and garnish immediately before serving. (See recipe, p. 41.)

One Day Before The Party:

- Peel the onions, slice the mushrooms, cut up the carrots, and chop the parsley for the *Cornish Game Hens en Casserole*. Refrigerate them separately in tightly sealed plastic bags until you're ready to make the dish. At the same time, season and truss the hens; refrigerate them in plastic bags or in a tightly covered container so they don't dry out. (See recipe, p. 55.)
- Cook the rices for *Double-Wild Rice*; clean, trim, and quarter the mushrooms. When it's time to prepare the dish, reheat the combined rices in the microwave or in a steamer while you sauté the mushrooms, then proceed with the recipe. (See recipe, p. 120.)
- Peel and section the grapefruit for the *Arugula, Grapefruit, and Goat Cheese Salad*; wash and thoroughly dry the arugula. Refrigerate separately in tightly sealed plastic bags. Make the dressing and store in a covered container. Immediately before serving, assemble and dress the salad. (See recipe, p. 31.)

The Evening of the Party:

- Right before your guests are scheduled to arrive, finish preparing the *New Potatoes with Dill*.
- Arrange assorted cheeses and crackers on serving platter; set out *Herbed Olives*.
- Approximately 45 minutes before you plan to serve dinner, proceed with the *Cornish Game Hens En Casserole* and start it simmering so it will be ready when the soup course is over.
- About 15 minutes before you plan to serve dinner, finish preparing the rice and set it aside to keep warm.
- As your guests are being seated at the table, season and garnish soup and serve.
- After the soup course, serve the casserole and rice together. Assemble the salad, and serve separately, after the main course.
- Serve the *Peach Tart* and coffee or tea.

Cornish Game Hens en Casserole (see p. 54),
Double-Wild Rice (see p. 120), and *Arugula,*
Grapefruit, and Goat Cheese Salad (see p. 31).

FISH AND SHELLFISH

The felicitous combination of quick cooking and highly polyunsaturated fats makes fish and shellfish a fitting entree for today's cook.

Although seafood is best when bought fresh and eaten the same day, keeping some on hand in the freezer or in cans on your pantry shelf makes serving fish two or three times a week easy to do. Canned tuna and salmon form a nutritional basis for quick or last-minute meals. Canned clams can be added to pastas, soups, and dips, and clam broth is a good substitute for fish stock.

To retain flavor and nutritional value, poaching is one of the preferred cooking techniques. Fillets, steaks, or even an entire fish are placed in a poacher with warm, *not hot*, seasoned water or fish stock to cover, then simmered until tender—from 5 to 30 minutes depending on the thickness of the fish. If you don't have a fish poacher, however, you can use a large, deep, nonstick skillet with a lid. (If you're poaching a whole fish that is too big for the skillet, simply cut it in half and reassemble after cooking.) Tuna, sole, salmon, trout, halibut, bass, cod, and orange roughy are particularly well suited to poaching.

Poach it, broil it, bake it, steam it—whatever your method of preparation, make it a habit to enjoy fish and shellfish frequently.

BUYING GUIDE FOR FRESH FISH AND SHELLFISH

Fish should:

- Have clear, bulging eyes.

- Look moist and have a glossy sheen.

- Look firm, not soggy—flesh should spring back when pressed.

- Smell sweet or "briny," never "fishy."

- Scales should be firmly attached.

- Fish steaks and fillets should not be dry or brown at the edges.

- Shrimp and scallops should be very firm, with a sweet, mild odor.

- The shells of oysters, mussels, and clams should be tightly closed.

- Live lobsters should be active, not sluggish.

The Canadian Fisheries Cooking Theory is a good rule-of-thumb to follow. Cook fish 10 minutes for every inch of thickness. Measure the fish at its thickest part.

Broiled Salmon with White and Black-Bean Salad,
see p. 65.

Peppered Tuna Steak
with Tomato Coulis

Serve this, and your friends might think there's a chef hiding in your kitchen. No one need know how easy it is.

INGREDIENTS:
1 teaspoon black peppercorns
1 teaspoon white peppercorns
1 teaspoon pink peppercorns
1 teaspoon green peppercorns
4 1-inch-thick tuna steaks, about 6 to 8 ounces each
Salt to taste
10 tablespoons olive oil
1 teaspoon minced garlic
1 shallot, coarsely chopped
4 large beefsteak tomatoes, peeled, seeded, and diced *or*
8 Italian plum tomatoes, peeled, seeded, and diced

EQUIPMENT:
2-quart saucepan
Food processor or blender
12-inch sauté pan or *sautôir*

Crack peppercorns by pressing them on a hard surface with the bottom of a heavy saucepan. Mix together cracked peppercorns and press firmly into both sides of each tuna steak with the heel of your hand. Sprinkle lightly with salt and set aside.

To make the coulis, heat 4 tablespoons of the olive oil in saucepan and sauté garlic and shallot about 2 minutes over low heat. Add diced tomatoes, raise heat to medium, and cook for 5 minutes, stirring occasionally. Allow to cool slightly, then place in container of food processor or blender and puree.

To sauté pan add the remaining 6 tablespoons of olive oil and heat until smoking. Add the steaks and sear over high heat for 2 minutes to a side. Lower heat and cook 10 minutes more, or until fish is white throughout.

Ladle the coulis in equal amounts onto 4 dinner plates and place the tuna steaks on top. **Serves 4.**

> TO PEEL TOMATOES, drop in boiling water to cover for 1 to 2 minutes in order to loosen the skin, then place immediately in ice water to stop the cooking. Remove and peel skin with small knife.

Peppered Tuna Steak with Tomato Coulis

BLACK-EYED PEA AND TUNA CASSEROLE

The infamous tuna-noodle-mushroom soup casserole of yore makes today's sophisticated, diet-conscious cook cringe. But water-packed canned tuna is relatively low in calories, high in nutrition, and can still be the basis of quick, easy, delicious (and inexpensive) main dishes.

INGREDIENTS:

2 tablespoons olive oil
⅔ cup minced scallions, white and tender greens
2 cups dried black-eyed peas, soaked and cooked until tender according to package directions
3 Italian plum tomatoes, chopped
2 tablespoons tomato paste
½ teaspoon red pepper flakes
2 (6-ounce) cans water-packed white tuna, drained and broken into chunks
Salt and freshly ground black pepper to taste
½ cup bread crumbs
¼ cup grated Romano cheese

EQUIPMENT:

8-inch sauté pan
2½-quart covered casserole
Small (1-quart) mixing bowl

Preheat oven to 350°. Heat olive oil in sauté pan over medium heat and sauté scallions 2 to 3 minutes, stirring constantly. Place cooked peas in oiled casserole and add sautéed scallions, tomatoes, tomato paste, red pepper flakes, and tuna. Season with salt and pepper and toss gently to blend. Cover and bake 25 minutes. In bowl, mix together bread crumbs and cheese. Remove casserole cover, stir tuna, then sprinkle with bread-cheese mixture. Raise oven temperature to 400° and bake 5 minutes uncovered, or until crumb cover is golden brown. **Serves 4 to 6.** ● ■

FRESH TUNA BAKED IN FOIL

INGREDIENTS:

2 tablespoons butter or margarine
2 medium onions, coarsely chopped
3 garlic cloves, minced
8 medium mushrooms, trimmed and coarsely chopped
4 1-inch-thick tuna steaks, about 6 ounces each
4 tablespoons finely chopped fresh Italian flat-leaf parsley
Salt and freshly ground black pepper to taste
1 cup dry white wine

EQUIPMENT:

10-inch sauté pan
Baking sheet

Preheat oven to 350°. In sauté pan, melt butter and cook onions and garlic over medium heat 3 minutes; add mushrooms and continue cooking 5 to 7 minutes more, stirring occasionally.

Place each tuna steak on a large square of heavy-duty aluminum foil. Fold up edges of foil slightly to form a dish shape. Spoon ¼ of vegetable mixture on top of each tuna steak, sprinkle with parsley, salt, and pepper, and pour ¼ cup of white wine over each. Form a tent around the fish with the foil and seal tightly. Place on baking sheet and bake 15 to 20 minutes. Tuna should be white and opaque all the way through and flake easily with a fork. Do not overbake. Serve in tents that are opened by diners. **Serves 4.** ● ■

TIP: Foods cooked in foil—with the exception of chicken—require longer cooking times.

TIP: This dish can also be baked in foil outdoors on a charcoal grill. Prepare as instructed, then place on grill 3 inches above hot coals for 20 minutes.

BROILED SALMON WITH WHITE- AND BLACK-BEAN SALAD

A dinner party treat—simple enough to make every day.

INGREDIENTS:
¾ cup dried black beans
¾ cup dried white kidney beans (cannellini)
2 quarts boiling water
3 large garlic cloves, crushed
⅔ cup olive oil
4 salmon fillets, 6 ounces each, skin removed
Salt and freshly ground black or white pepper to taste
1 tablespoon fresh lemon juice
2 tablespoons chopped fresh chives

EQUIPMENT:
2 2½-quart covered saucepans
Colander
Large (4-quart) mixing bowl
Shallow roasting pan with rack

TIP: If you're tempted to cook beans in the same pot, *don't!* The water in which the black beans are cooked turns as black as ink and will turn the white beans gray.

Place black beans in one saucepan, white beans in the other; add 1 quart boiling water to each and, after water returns to a boil, reduce heat to medium and cook, covered, 20 to 30 minutes. Remove from heat and let stand, covered, 30 minutes more. Drain beans in colander and rinse with cold water. Place in bowl, add garlic and ½ cup of olive oil, and mix well. Then cover and marinate 4 to 6 hours or overnight in the refrigerator.

Twenty minutes before serving, remove beans from refrigerator and preheat oven to Broil. Add lemon juice, salt, pepper, and chives to beans and mix well. Arrange 4 equal portions on dinner plates.

Brush salmon on both sides with some of the remaining olive oil and season with salt and pepper. Brush rack of broiling pan with the rest of the olive oil, place fillets on rack in pan and cook under broiler about 5 minutes. Turn fillets and cook 5 minutes more. Remove from oven. Place one fillet on top of beans on each plate and serve immediately. **Serves 4.**

See photo, p. 60.

MARINATED BROILED TROUT

INGREDIENTS:
6 whole brook trout, about 1 pound each, cleaned
⅓ cup olive oil
⅓ cup fresh lemon juice
1 tablespoon fresh thyme leaves or 1 teaspoon dried thyme
Salt and freshly ground black pepper to taste
¼ cup chopped fresh Italian flat-leaf parsley

EQUIPMENT:
Shallow glass or ceramic baking dish
Small bowl or 2-cup measuring cup
Shallow roasting pan

Place trout in baking dish. Combine olive oil, lemon juice, thyme, salt, and pepper in bowl. Pour marinade over fish. Cover and refrigerate 2 hours, basting occasionally. Turn fish after 1 hour. Pour off and reserve marinade. Place trout in roasting pan. Broil 4 to 6 inches from heat 4 minutes per side or until flesh is opaque, basting every 2 minutes with the marinade. Garnish with parsley. **Serves 6.**

VARIATION: Substitute ⅓ cup fresh lime juice for the lemon juice and 1 tablespoon chopped fresh cilantro for the thyme.

TROUT AMANDINE

INGREDIENTS:
4 brook or rainbow trout, about 10 ounces each,
   cleaned and heads removed
Salt and freshly ground black pepper to taste
Flour for dredging, about ½ cup
6 tablespoons safflower or soy oil
6 ounces unsalted butter
½ cup sliced, blanched almonds
½ cup fresh lemon juice
¼ cup chopped fresh Italian flat-leaf parsley

EQUIPMENT:
Pie plate
10-inch sauté pan

Sprinkle trout with salt and pepper; dredge with flour, shaking off excess. Heat sauté pan over high heat until very hot and add half the oil. Lower heat to medium. Place 2 trout in pan and sauté 3 to 5 minutes until golden brown. Turn fish and sauté 5 minutes more to brown other side. Remove from pan and set aside to keep warm. Add remaining oil to pan and cook remaining trout. Remove from pan and set aside.

Pour off oil and wipe out pan. Return to heat, add butter and almonds, and cook until lightly browned. Add lemon juice, parsley, salt, and pepper, stirring to blend, about 1 minute. Pour almond sauce over trout and serve. **Serves 4.** ● ■

HALIBUT WITH CONFETTI SAUCE

INGREDIENTS:
4 halibut steaks, about 6 ounces each
½ cup fresh lemon juice
Salt and freshly ground black or white pepper to
   taste
¼ cup chopped scallions, white and tender
   greens
2 cups shredded carrots
¼ cup chopped fresh Italian flat-leaf parsley
3 tablespoons chopped fresh dill
2 large tomatoes, peeled and chopped
½ cup bean sprouts or julienned cucumber
1 lemon, cut in wedges

EQUIPMENT:
4-quart covered casserole or
   15 × 10 × 2-inch baking dish
Medium (2½-quart) mixing bowl

Preheat oven to 350°. Place halibut in baking dish and season with lemon juice, salt, and pepper. In bowl, toss together scallions, carrots, parsley, and dill and spoon over fish. Cover and bake 20 minutes or until fish flakes with a fork. Garnish with chopped tomato, bean sprouts or cucumber, and lemon wedges. **Serves 4.** ● ■

CREAMY NONDAIRY PIMENTO SAUCE
This sauce is simple to prepare and terrific over fish.

INGREDIENTS:
1 (12-ounce) container soft tofu, drained
1 (6-ounce) can whole pimentos, drained
1 teaspoon or more ground cumin
1 teaspoon or more paprika
1 to 2 garlic cloves, peeled
2 tablespoons cider vinegar
1 tablespoon olive oil
2 tablespoons Worcestershire sauce
2 tablespoons capers, drained
1 tablespoon fresh lemon juice
6 to 8 small sun-dried tomatoes, reconstituted in
   boiling water for 3 minutes and drained
½ cup toasted almonds (optional)

EQUIPMENT:
Food processor or blender
2-quart saucepan

Place all ingredients in food processor and blend until very smooth. Allow to stand 1 hour to blend flavors. Taste and correct seasoning, then heat in a saucepan over medium-low heat. **Yield: about 3 cups.** ● ■

Halibut with Confetti Sauce

Hot Snapper Veracruz

Serve this spicy snapper over white rice to absorb the delicious juices. Cool down with Minted Cucumber Salad (see p. 25) and a classically simple steamed or sautéed zucchini dish.

INGREDIENTS:

4 red snapper fillets, about 6 ounces each
Juice of 3 to 4 limes
3 tablespoons olive oil
2 garlic cloves, minced
1 onion, chopped
3 to 4 small tomatoes, chopped
1 or 2 jalapeño peppers, seeded and finely
  chopped
Salt and freshly ground black pepper to taste
⅓ cup chopped fresh cilantro leaves

EQUIPMENT:

9 × 13-inch baking dish
8-inch sauté pan

Place fish in greased baking dish. Add lime juice to nearly cover and marinate 30 minutes, turning fillets once. In sauté pan, heat oil over medium-high heat; add garlic and onion and sauté 3 to 4 minutes. Add tomatoes and jalapeños and simmer gently 5 minutes. Preheat oven to 350°. Spread tomato sauce over fish (leave lime-juice marinade in pan) and sprinkle with cilantro. Cover and bake 20 minutes or until fish flakes with a fork. **Serves 4.**
● ■

TIP: To avoid contact with skin, wear rubber gloves when peparing jalapeños.

Mustard-Broiled Swordfish
with Fresh Dill

INGREDIENTS:

2 1-inch-thick swordfish steaks, about 1 pound
  each
Salt and freshly ground black pepper to taste
3 tablespoons coarse-grained mustard
3 tablespoons butter or margarine, melted
Finely chopped fresh dill for garnish

EQUIPMENT:

9 × 13-inch baking pan

Preheat oven to Broil. Sprinkle swordfish steaks with salt and pepper on both sides, then brush both sides with mustard. Cover bottom of baking dish with melted butter; place steaks in dish and broil 4 to 5 minutes. Turn steaks and broil 4 to 5 minutes more. Do not overcook or fish will become dry. Cut steaks in half, sprinkle with fresh dill, and serve. **Serves 4.**

Chinese Sea Bass

CHINESE SEA BASS

INGREDIENTS:
2 tablespoons peanut oil
2 tablespoons sesame seeds
1 tablespoon minced fresh ginger
2 garlic cloves, minced
2 scallions, white and tender greens, minced
3 tablespoons soy sauce
3 tablespoons dry white wine
2 whole sea bass, 1 to 1½ pounds each, cleaned
4 tablespoons finely chopped fresh cilantro leaves

EQUIPMENT:
10-inch sauté pan
Deep roasting pan with rack

Preheat oven to 400°. Heat oil in sauté pan over high heat and sauté sesame seeds until golden, about 1 minute. Add ginger, garlic, scallions, and cook, stirring constantly, 2 to 3 minutes, until scallions are barely wilted. Add soy sauce and wine, lower heat, and simmer 1 minute.

Place fish on rack in roasting pan; pour half the sauce over it and bake 10 minutes. Pour remaining sauce over fish and bake 5 more minutes, or until fish flakes easily with a fork. Transfer to serving platter, sprinkle with cilantro, and serve. **Serves 4.**

FILLET OF SOLE
WITH TOMATOES AND PARSLEY

INGREDIENTS:
1 tablespoon olive oil
4 medium tomatoes, chopped
1 small onion, chopped
1 garlic clove, minced
½ cup dry white wine
2 tablespoons fresh lemon juice
4 fillets of sole, about 6 ounces each
¼ cup minced Italian flat-leaf parsley
¼ teaspoon dried oregano
Salt and freshly ground black pepper to taste

EQUIPMENT:
10-inch sauté pan
4-quart (15 × 10 × 2-inch) baking dish or casserole

Preheat oven to 350°. Heat olive oil in sauté pan and sauté tomatoes, onion, and garlic for 10 minutes, or until wilted. Add wine and cook to reduce by one half. Stir in lemon juice. Arrange fillets in a layer in greased baking dish. Pour tomato mixture over fish, sprinkle with parsley, oregano, salt, and pepper. Bake 12 to 15 minutes or until fish flakes with a fork. Serve with rice. **Serves 4.** ● ■

Fillet of Sole with Tomatoes and Parsley

Fisherman's Supper

FISHERMAN'S SUPPER

A one-dish fish meal that only takes about 15 minutes to prepare and makes a perfect family dinner.

INGREDIENTS:
4 tablespoons olive oil
6 medium-size new potatoes, scrubbed, sliced into eighths
3 large yellow onions, cut into ¼-inch slices
3 medium green or red bell peppers, cored, seeded, and sliced into eighths
2½ pounds sea trout fillet or other firm-fleshed fish such as orange roughy or monk fish, cut into 2-inch pieces
Salt and freshly ground black pepper to taste

EQUIPMENT:
4-quart covered casserole

Preheat oven to 350°. Spread oil evenly on the bottom of casserole. Add potatoes, onions, peppers, fish, and seasonings; cover dish and bake 20 minutes. Remove cover, raise heat to 400°, stir gently, and bake 10 to 15 more minutes, or until fish and vegetables begin to brown. **Serves 6.** ● ■

SIMPLY STEAMED SEAFOOD

Serve with pasta tossed with olive oil, buttered rice, orzo, or couscous.

INGREDIENTS:
8 hard-shell clams, cherrystones or littlenecks
24 to 30 large mussels
1 pound medium shrimp, shelled and deveined
1 pound sea scallops
1 onion, coarsely chopped
1 bunch fresh Italian flat-leaf parsley, chopped
1 cup dry white wine

EQUIPMENT:
9 × 13-inch glass or ceramic baking dish or
    3-quart covered casserole

Scrub clams and place in cold water to cover for at least 1 hour before cooking. Examine clams and mussels and discard any that are cracked or not tightly closed. Scrub mussels thoroughly under running water, pulling out and discarding fiberlike "beards." Preheat oven to 400°. Put all shellfish in baking dish; cover with onion and parsley; pour white wine over top. If baking dish has no lid, seal tightly with foil. Bake for 15 to 20 minutes, or until clams and mussels open, scallops become opaque, and shrimp turn pink. **Serves 4.**

TIP: If you shell the shrimp yourself, see page 43 for instructions on making a shrimp broth.

SHRIMP AND FETA

INGREDIENTS:
1½ pounds medium shrimp
½ cup dry white wine
½ cup water
8 tablespoons olive oil
1 onion, finely chopped
3 garlic cloves, minced
1 (28-ounce) can Italian plum tomatoes, drained
    and broken up with a fork
1 teaspoon dried oregano
2 tablespoons capers, drained
Salt and freshly ground black pepper to taste
½ pound feta cheese, crumbled

EQUIPMENT:
1½ quart saucepan
2½-quart saucepan
12-inch sauté pan or sautôir
Shallow 2½-quart casserole

Peel shrimp and add shells to small saucepan. Devein shrimp and refrigerate covered. Add wine and water to shells in pan. Bring to a boil then simmer briskly until liquid is reduced to half. Discard shells. Preheat oven to 350°. Heat 5 tablespoons olive oil in medium saucepan over medium heat; add onions and garlic; sauté 2 minutes. Add tomatoes shrimp broth, oregano, capers, salt, and pepper. Bring to a boil over high heat, then reduce heat to medium and simmer 25 to 30 minutes or until slightly thickened, stirring frequently.

Heat remaining 3 tablespoons olive oil in sauté pan and add shrimp, stirring and turning for 2 to 3 minutes, or until they turn pink. *Do not overcook.* If you use a smaller sauté pan, you may have to do this in two batches.

Spread half the sauce over the bottom of casserole. Arrange shrimp on top and cover with remaining sauce. Scatter crumbled cheese evenly on top and bake 10 to 15 minutes. **Serves 6.**

COOKING YOGURT: Yogurt curdles easily when cooked. To prevent curdling, mix 1 tablespoon cornstarch with 1 tablespoon yogurt; blend with remaining yogurt. However, take care not to boil.

SHRIMP MADRAS

INGREDIENTS:
2 pounds fresh shrimp, shelled and deveined
1 tablespoon chopped fresh mint leaves
2 teaspoons turmeric
½ teaspoon ground coriander
1 teaspoon grated fresh ginger or ½ teaspoon
    powdered ginger
2 garlic cloves, minced
½ teaspoon ground cumin
4 tablespoons vegetable oil
1 medium-size onion, grated
1 tablespoon cornstarch
1 cup plain yogurt
2 tablespoons chopped fresh Italian flat-leaf
    parsley or cilantro leaves
Juice of ½ lemon
Salt and freshly ground black pepper to taste

EQUIPMENT:
Large (4-quart) mixing bowl
12-inch sauté pan or *sautôir*
Small bowl or 2-cup measuring cup

Place shrimp in bowl; add next 6 ingredients and mix well by hand until all shrimp are coated. Let stand 1 hour.

Heat 3 tablespoons oil in sauté pan. Add grated onion (chopped onion will not work as well) and cook, stirring, until onion is fairly dry without browning. Add remaining oil and shrimp mixture. Stirring and gently turning, cook shrimp until they start to turn pink. Mix cornstarch with one tablespoon yogurt in bowl, add to the remaining yogurt and add to pan. Simmer very gently on low heat 10 more minutes. Add parsley, lemon juice, and salt and pepper to taste. Serve with rice. **Serves 6.**

Shrimp Madras

CURRIED SCALLOPS

INGREDIENTS:
3 tablespoons butter or margarine
2 shallots, chopped
2 pounds whole bay or quartered sea scallops
2 cups dry white wine
1½ teaspoons chopped fresh thyme leaves or ½
    teaspoon dried thyme
1 tablespoon curry powder
½ cup plain yogurt
1 tablespoon cornstarch

EQUIPMENT:
3-quart saucepan
Small bowl or 2-cup measuring cup

Melt butter in saucepan over medium heat; sauté shallots for 5 minutes, add scallops, and cook 1 minute. Add wine, thyme, and curry powder; cover, then reduce heat and simmer 5 minutes. *Do not overcook.* With slotted spoon, remove scallops to warmed serving dish. Raise heat to bring liquid to a boil and cook until reduced by half. Lower heat, combine 1 tablespoon of the yogurt and cornstarch, and blend with remaining yogurt. Add to sauce; heat, stirring, for 2 minutes. Pour sauce over scallops and serve. **Serves 6.** ● ■

Curried Scallops

Beef, Bean, and Corn Chili (see p. 79), and *Colorful Salad (see p. 28).*

CASUAL DINNER FOR FRIENDS

Yogurt Aioli with Crudités
Colorful Salad
Beef, Bean, and Corn Chili
Chocolate Angel-Food Cake

A small gathering of favorite friends is probably the most enjoyable kind of dinner party to put together. You don't have to deplete your energy preparing elegant dishes or waste precious time on a flashy presentation—these are your friends, after all, and they simply expect good chow and some laughs. You probably don't need an excuse to assemble this crowd, though the Super Bowl, the Oscars, or Elvis's birthday are good ones.

The hardest part—which we've done for you—is to think of something yummy to make that can be prepared ahead of time and served in an uncomplicated manner. You don't want to be sifting, sautéing, and flambéing in the kitchen while your friends are having all the fun in the living room.

Cold appetizers are a good place to start. An appealing but simple salad can be assembled before your guests arrive and tossed with the dressing at the last minute. A big pot of chili is always a great idea—it can even be prepared a day ahead of time and reheated just before serving. A light bake-ahead cake for dessert will bring on the final applause for your efforts (or your seeming lack of effort).

TIMETABLE

Two Days Before:

- Shop for all your ingredients.
- Buy any beverages and related items, lemons, limes, mixers, etc., you'll require.

The Night Before:

- Prepare the *Beef, Bean, and Corn Chili*, but don't include the corn. You will add the corn when you're reheating the chili before serving. (See recipe, p. 79.)
- Once the chili is assembled and simmering, put the head of garlic in the oven to bake for the *Yogurt Aioli*. After the garlic is baked, assemble the dip and refrigerate in a well-sealed container. (See recipe, p. 16.)
- Prepare the *Chocolate Angel-Food Cake*. Let it cool and store in a cake saver or loosely covered with foil or plastic wrap. (See recipe, p. 152.)

The Morning Before:

- Wash and prepare your vegetables for the crudités. Store them separately in airtight plastic bags until ready to serve.
- Wash and pat dry the romaine lettuce for the *Colorful Salad*. Store the lettuce leaves sandwiched between sheets of paper towel in airtight plastic bags. Clean and chop the cilantro for the salad and store it in a plastic bag or container in the refrigerator. Prepare the dressing. (See recipe, p. 28.)

An Hour Before:

- Finish assembling the *Colorful Salad*. Do not toss with dressing until just before serving. Cover with plastic wrap and store in the refrigerator.
- Prepare toppings for chili (grated cheese, sour cream, chopped cilantro, scallions, bell peppers or tomatoes, and crushed tortilla chips) and place in separate bowls. Cover with plastic wrap and chill until ready to serve.
- Set a table buffet-style, with dinner plates, soup bowls, salad plates, dessert plates, silverware (including soup spoons), and a variety of colorful cloth napkins.

Fifteen Minutes Before:

- Place *Yogurt Aioli* in serving bowl and arrange with the crudités on a serving tray.
- Set up your mini-bar (glasses, a bucket of ice, tongs, twists, mixers, napkins) in a convenient place. Keep chilled beverages in the refrigerator until the guests begin to arrive, then bring them out as needed.
- Get your music selections in order, go change clothes, brush your teeth, and pinch your cheeks.

After Guests Arrive:

- Set out the appetizer where your guests are assembled and make sure everyone has a beverage. Begin reheating the chili on medium-low; add the corn. Toss the salad with the dressing and set it out on the buffet table, along with the toppings for the chili and the *Chocolate Angel-Food Cake*.
- Then relax and enjoy your own party. Everything else will pretty much take care of itself— you'll find everyone is happy to get their own beverages and help themselves to dinner. (Don't forget to set out the chili on a warming tray or trivet after it has reheated for ½ hour.) And there's always some eager beaver egging you on to cut the cake.

MEATS

Red meat has taken a lot of heat in recent decades. We have all been warned that we eat too much of it—but there is no need to eliminate it from your diet completely.

To follow a healthy eating plan that includes red meat there are several steps that you can take. First of all, rethink your serving sizes, and don't make meat the largest portion on your plate. Try 3- or 4-ounce servings instead of the typical 6- to 8-ounce portions that most Americans consume. Fill out your menu with soup as a first course and more vegetables, grains, and legumes as side dishes.

Trim off all excess fat, preferably before but certainly after cooking. Buy choice, lean cuts and become familiar with the fat content of different cuts. Always buy *lean* ground meats. Regular ground beef, for example, has as much as 30 percent more fat than lean. Finally, serve red meat occasionally rather than frequently.

SWEDISH MEATBALLS

INGREDIENTS:
½ cup soft fresh bread crumbs
½ cup milk
3 tablespoons butter or margarine
3 tablespoons finely chopped onion
1 egg, beaten
½ teaspoon allspice
½ teaspoon Tabasco sauce
Salt and freshly ground black pepper to taste
1 pound lean ground beef
½ pound lean ground pork
1 tablespoon flour
1 cup light cream

EQUIPMENT:
Large (4-quart) mixing bowl
10-inch skillet

Combine bread crumbs and milk in large mixing bowl; set aside. Heat 1 tablespoon butter over medium heat in skillet, add onions, and sauté until soft. Add egg, allspice, ¼ teaspoon Tabasco, salt, pepper, sautéed onions, beef, and pork to bread crumbs. Mix well by hand and shape into 36 balls.

Heat remaining butter in skillet over medium-high heat; add meatballs, turning to cook evenly and brown lightly. Set cooked meatballs aside on heated platter. Add flour, remaining Tabasco, and cream to skillet and stir over medium heat until mixture thickens to consistency of gravy; salt and pepper to taste. Serve meatballs on a bed of rice or egg noodles; pour gravy over meat. **Serves 4 to 6.**

SHISH KEBAB is probably the most common dish in Eastern European and Russian cuisine. The item grilled on the skewer depends on the recipe's region of origin. For instance, Turks and Armenians most often feature lamb, while Russians primarily grill beef in this manner. Chicken and sturgeon also show up on the skewer in some areas. All of it seems like a good idea to us, so go ahead and improvise with whatever you've got available.

Lamb Kebabs,
see p. 86.

Steak au Poivre

STEAK AU POIVRE

INGREDIENTS:
4 shell steaks, 6 ounces each
3 tablespoons very coarsely ground black pepper
Salt to taste
5 tablespoons vegetable oil
1 teaspoon whole pink peppercorns, crushed
1 tablespoon whole green peppercorns, crushed
4 tablespoons coarsely chopped shallots
1 cup cognac or brandy
1⅔ cups beef or veal broth, canned or homemade
1½ cups heavy cream
Salt and freshly ground black pepper to taste

EQUIPMENT:
2½-quart saucepan
12-inch skillet or *sautôir*

Sprinkle both sides of each steak with black pepper. With heel of hand, press pepper firmly into meat. Salt to taste and set aside.

To prepare sauce, heat 2 tablespoons of oil in saucepan. Cook pink and green peppercorns and shallots over low heat until shallots are wilted but not browned. Remove pan well away from heat and add cognac or brandy. Return pan to burner, ignite cognac with a match, and cook until the flame goes out. Add broth and cook until mixture is reduced by half. Add cream and continue cooking, stirring constantly, until mixture is thick enough to coat the back of a spoon. Season to taste with salt and pepper and set aside to keep warm.

With burner on high, heat skillet or *sautôir* until very hot. Add enough of remaining oil to cover bottom of pan. Add 2 steaks, all 4 if pan is large enough, searing just until nicely browned. Turn steaks and cook approximately 2 minutes longer for medium rare. Remove from pan and keep warm while cooking remaining steaks. Pour sauce over steaks and serve immediately. **Serves 4.**

BEEF, BEAN, AND CORN CHILI

INGREDIENTS:

3 tablespoons vegetable oil
2 pounds top round steak, trimmed of fat and cut into ½-inch cubes
3 Spanish onions, coarsely chopped
1 pound dried pinto beans, soaked
¼ cup fine-quality chili powder
2 teaspoons ground cumin
Salt and freshly ground black pepper to taste
3 garlic cloves, mashed
2 cups canned crushed tomatoes
6 cups water
2 to 3 jalapeño peppers, seeded and finely chopped
4 small cans, about 2 ounces each, mild green chilies, coarsely chopped
2 teaspoons dried oregano
3 cups fresh corn kernels, about 5 cobs, or frozen corn kernels, thawed

EQUIPMENT:

8-quart Dutch oven or stockpot

ZESTY MEAT LOAF

This "one-step-prep" recipe is about as easy as recipes can get.

INGREDIENTS:

1 pound lean ground beef
12 ounces beef or pork sausage in bulk
1 medium onion, coarsely chopped
½ green bell pepper, cored, seeded, and coarsely chopped
⅔ cup bread crumbs, fresh or dried
1 egg, lightly beaten
3 tablespoons catsup
2 tablespoons prepared brown mustard
Salt and freshly ground black pepper to taste
½ teaspoon dried thyme
½ teaspoon dried sage
¼ teaspoon cayenne pepper (optional)

EQUIPMENT:

Large (4-quart) mixing bowl
1½-quart loaf pan

Preheat oven to 350°. Combine all ingredients in bowl and mix thoroughly. Place in loaf pan and bake 45 minutes. **Serves 6.**

Heat oil in Dutch oven over high heat and brown beef, being careful not to crowd pieces. Do in several batches if necessary. Add onions and cook for 10 minutes. Reduce heat; add remaining ingredients except corn and simmer for 2 to 3 hours, the longer the better. Add corn 15 minutes before serving. **Serves 8.**

TIP: Serve with a variety of toppings on the side: grated Cheddar or Monterey Jack cheese, sour cream, chopped fresh cilantro, jicama slices, chopped scallions, tortilla chips, guacamole, rice, chopped bell peppers, or chopped fresh tomatoes.

Beef, Bean, and Corn Chili

Moroccan Pockets

MOROCCAN POCKETS

A great informal supper dish. Serve with a green salad.

INGREDIENTS:
1 pound lean ground beef
1 large onion, chopped
1 cup cored, seeded, and chopped green bell
   pepper
1 garlic clove, mashed
1 (16-ounce) can peeled tomatoes, undrained
2 tablespoons chili powder
1 teaspoon ground cumin
1 teaspoon dried oregano
1 cup pearl barley
1½ cups water
1 cup raisins
Salt and freshly ground black pepper to taste
4 large pita breads
¼ cup chopped fresh Italian flat-leaf parsley
1 pint plain yogurt

EQUIPMENT:
10-inch skillet
2½-quart covered saucepan

Brown beef over medium-high heat in skillet, breaking up lumps with spoon. Add onion, green pepper, and garlic and cook until onion is limp. Drain off fat. Place meat mixture in saucepan and add tomatoes, chili powder, cumin, oregano, barley, and water. Cover and simmer 35 to 40 minutes, or until barley is tender. Stir in raisins and salt and pepper to taste.

To serve, cut pita bread in half, making "pockets." Spoon beef mixture into the bread. Stir parsley into yogurt and use to top filling. **Serves 4.**

Cabbage Rolls

CABBAGE ROLLS

This recipe serves 8. If you're serving fewer than that, don't reduce the recipe—cabbage rolls taste even better the next day. They can also be cooked ahead of time and stored in the freezer. Serve over rice.

INGREDIENTS:
2 heads green cabbage, cored
2 pounds lean ground beef
1 large onion, chopped
Paprika to taste
2 (16-ounce) bottles chili sauce
¼ cup firmly packed brown sugar, light or dark
¼ cup fresh lemon juice
1 cup raisins
Salt and freshly ground black pepper to taste

EQUIPMENT:
6-quart stockpot
Large (4-quart) mixing bowl
4½-quart Dutch oven

Wrapping *Cabbage Rolls*

Gently boil each cabbage head in stockpot about 10 to 15 minutes, until leaves are tender enough to separate. Remove and let cool. In bowl, mix together beef, onion, and paprika. Separate cabbage leaves and drain well. Place 2 to 4 tablespoons (depending on size of leaf) firmly packed meat mixture on center of each cabbage leaf. Wrap leaves around meat as shown in the photo. Layer cabbage rolls in Dutch oven; the pan should be about ⅔ full. Pour chili sauce over top, add remaining ingredients (no need to mix ingredients). Gently simmer, covered, over very low heat 2 to 3 hours. Season with salt and pepper and serve. **Serves 8.**

Veal Escallops with Lime

VEAL ESCALLOPS WITH LIME

INGREDIENTS:
16 thin veal cutlets, about 1¼ pounds total
4 to 6 tablespoons olive oil
Salt and freshly ground black pepper to taste
1 bunch fresh basil, leaves chopped
Juice of 2 limes

EQUIPMENT:
12-inch skillet

Flatten cutlets with a meat pounder. Add 2 tablespoons of the oil to pan and heat. Add as many cutlets as will fit at a time and sauté over high heat. Season to taste with salt and pepper. Cook for 45 seconds on each side, remove from pan and cover to keep warm. Repeat with remaining cutlets, adding olive oil as needed. A minute before serving, sprinkle with fresh basil and lime juice. **Serves 4.**

NEW ENGLAND BOILED DINNER

INGREDIENTS:
1 lean corned-beef brisket or ham butt, about 4
   pounds, trimmed of all excess fat
1 large rutabaga, peeled, cut into 8 equal-sized
   pieces
3 small parsnips, peeled, cut in 2-inch lengths
6 medium carrots, peeled, cut in 2-inch lengths
8 small red new potatoes, unpeeled
4 large leeks, white and 2 inches of tender green,
   sliced in half lengthwise
1 medium head green cabbage, cored and cut
   into 8 wedges
Freshly ground black pepper to taste

EQUIPMENT:
8-quart covered Dutch oven or stockpot

Place corned beef or ham in stockpot, cover with boiling water and simmer corned beef over medium heat until fork-tender, about 2½ to 3 hours. Simmer ham butt 3 to 4 hours, or until internal temperature reaches 170° on a meat thermometer. Also with ham butt, skim off any scum that accumulates on surface during cooking.

Remove meat from stockpot; set aside. Add rutabaga, parsnips, carrots, and potatoes to pot, bring to boil, reduce heat, cover, and simmer about 20 minutes. Add leeks and cabbage wedges; simmer 10 more minutes. Return meat to stockpot; add pepper to taste and simmer approximately 15 minutes to reheat. Serve meat on a deep platter surrounded by vegetables; ladle some of the broth over all. **Serves 8.** ● ■

*Pork Chops
Baked in Wine*

PORK CHOPS BAKED IN WINE

Note that the alcohol in the wine marinade will completely evaporate as the meat cooks, leaving only the flavor.

INGREDIENTS:
4 lean center-cut pork chops, about 4 ounces
   each
½ cup Madeira wine
½ cup dry vermouth
¼ cup water
½ teaspoon dried thyme
Salt and freshly ground black pepper to taste
3 slices lemon
2 tablespoons minced onion

EQUIPMENT:
Shallow 4-quart covered glass/ceramic casserole
1-quart saucepan

Place the pork chops in casserole. In saucepan, combine all remaining ingredients except onion and bring to boil over medium heat. Lower heat and simmer 5 to 10 minutes. Add onion and simmer 1 to 2 more minutes. Remove from heat and let cool to room temperature. Pour marinade over chops and marinate 2 to 3 hours in refrigerator, turning occasionally.

Preheat oven to 350°. Take marinated chops from refrigerator, remove and discard lemon slices, turn meat once again, cover, and bake 10 minutes. Remove cover, baste, turn heat up to 400°. Bake 5 to 10 more minutes, or until chops are lightly browned. **Serves 4.**

ORIENTAL PORK STIR-FRY

Lean pork can be leaner than dark-meat chicken. Serve with sautéed watercress or bok choy.

INGREDIENTS:
3 tablespoons light sesame oil
8 to 10 garlic cloves, halved
1 pound boneless pork roast, loin or butt, sliced
   in very thin strips
4 to 6 scallions, white and tender greens,
   chopped
2 tablespoons fish sauce
Lots of freshly ground black pepper
1 tablespoon chopped fresh cilantro leaves

EQUIPMENT:
Wok or 10-inch skillet

Heat wok or skillet on high and add oil. Sauté garlic about 30 seconds; add pork. Cook, stirring constantly, about 5 minutes. Add remaining ingredients and stir-fry for another minute. Serve over white rice. **Serves 4.**

TIP: Fish sauce, found in most Oriental markets and many supermarkets, is a cooking staple in many Asian countries. Its distinct flavor is not at all "fishy" and wonderfully enhances the flavors of other ingredients.

Oriental Pork Stir-Fry

PORK ROAST WITH APRICOT SAUCE

INGREDIENTS:
2½ tablespoons soya or other mild-flavored oil
1¼ pound pork loin, boned (have your butcher
   do this)
¾ cup dry white wine
¾ cup chicken broth, canned or homemade
½ pound dried apricots, cut into small pieces
½ cup heavy cream
Salt and freshly ground black pepper to taste
2 tablespoons chopped fresh Italian flat-leaf
   parsley

EQUIPMENT:
10-inch skillet
Shallow roasting pan
2-quart saucepan

Preheat oven to 425°. In skillet, heat oil until smoking hot, then sear meat on all sides until golden brown. Transfer pork to roasting pan and roast about 20 minutes or until internal temperature reaches 160°.

While pork is roasting, make the sauce. Cook wine in saucepan over high heat and reduce to about ¼ cup. Add stock and apricots and reduce to about ⅔ cup. Add cream and continue cooking until mixture reaches a sauce consistency. Season to taste with salt and pepper and add parsley.

Remove pork from oven and let "rest" 15 minutes before carving into ¼-inch-thick slices. Arrange slices on serving platter and pour sauce over meat. **Serves 4.**

FESTIVE BAKED HAM

We give you recipes for two equally tasty glazes to choose from and
suggestions for colorful garnishes to go with each.

INGREDIENTS:
1 whole uncooked cured ham (or fresh ham), 10
  to 15 pounds (bone in)
1 recipe glaze (see below)

EQUIPMENT:
Deep roasting pan

See photo, p. 89.

Preheat oven to 350°. Using a sharp boning
knife, peel the tough skin from ham and trim off all
but a ¼-inch layer of fat. Score the fat with a knife
in a diamond pattern, then place ham in roasting
pan. Pour ⅓ of glaze over ham and bake 30 minutes. Remove ham from oven and pour remaining
glaze over it. Bake, basting frequently, for an additional 10 minutes per pound, or until a meat thermometer inserted into the thickest part away from
the bone registers 150 to 160°.

Remove ham from oven and let it rest about
15 minutes before transferring to warmed serving
platter, garnished according to suggestions provided with the glaze that you have selected.
Serves 8-10.

APPLE-CRANBERRY GLAZE

INGREDIENTS:
1 cup canned jellied cranberry sauce
½ cup apple jelly
¼ cup brown sugar, packed
1 cup apple juice

FOR GARNISH
Lady apples (tiny golf ball–size apples)
Red and green grapes

EQUIPMENT:
1-quart saucepan
Small bowl or 2-cup measuring cup

Place cranberry sauce and apple jelly in saucepan over low heat, stirring until melted. Combine
brown sugar and apple juice in small bowl and stir
until brown sugar is completely dissolved. Add to
melted cranberry-apple mixture and blend well.
Glaze and baste ham as indicated above. Decorate
platter with lady apples and bunches of red and
green grapes. **Yield: about 2½ cups.**

HONEY-MUSTARD GLAZE

INGREDIENTS:
Whole cloves
1¼ cups honey
½ cup white wine
¾ cup Dijon-style or spicy brown mustard

FOR GARNISH
Assorted fresh fruits (lady apples; seckel pears;
  kumquats; red, green, and black grapes, etc.)
Curly endive (chicory)

EQUIPMENT:
Small (1-quart) mixing bowl

Before baking ham, stud scored surface with
whole cloves, one clove per diamond. Combine
honey, wine, and mustard in small bowl and whisk
until thoroughly blended. Glaze and baste ham as
indicated above. Surround ham on serving platter
with a "Della Robbia wreath," composed of assorted
whole fresh fruits interspersed with curly endive.
Yield: about 2½ cups.

MOROCCAN LAMB BURGERS

These flavorful sandwiches feature curry or ground cumin and coriander—the staples of Moroccan cooking.

INGREDIENTS:
1 pound lean ground lamb
⅓ cup plain yogurt
1 egg, lightly beaten (optional)
1 teaspoon or more curry powder *or* ½ to 1
   teaspoon ground cumin and ¼ teaspoon ground
   coriander
Salt and freshly ground black pepper to taste
¼ cup finely chopped scallions, white and tender
   greens
3 tablespoons finely snipped "moist" dried
   apricots
1 to 2 tablespoons butter or margarine, (optional)
4 to 12 slices bread for patties, preferably oatmeal
   bread
Finely chopped chutney, plain yogurt, chopped
   fresh cilantro, or parsley for garnish (optional)

EQUIPMENT:
Medium (2½-quart) mixing bowl
Small (1-quart) mixing bowl
10-inch skillet

Place lamb in medium bowl. In smaller bowl, thoroughly mix together yogurt, egg (it helps to bind the mixture), and your choice of curry or cumin/coriander. Add salt and pepper and mix in scallions and apricots. Add this mixture to lamb, mix gently with moistened hands, then divide into 4 to 6 patties. Don't pack tightly.

Heat butter in skillet until it foams. Add patties and cook 3 to 5 minutes on a side. Lightly toast bread and serve closed or open faced with garnish and with thinly sliced cucumbers and cherry tomatoes on the side. **Serves 4 to 6.**

GRILLED LAMB KEBABS

INGREDIENTS:
½ cup olive oil
Juice of 1 lemon and grated zest
1 garlic clove, minced
1 tablespoon fresh rosemary sprigs or 1½
   teaspoons dried rosemary
1 tablespoon ground coriander
1 teaspoon salt
Several grinds of black pepper
2 pounds lamb, cut into 2-inch cubes

EQUIPMENT:
Large (4-quart) mixing bowl
Skewers

See photo, p. 76.

Mix first 7 ingredients in bowl. Add lamb and marinate in refrigerator 8 hours or overnight, turning occasionally. Drain lamb and place on skewers. Reserve marinade. Grill over hot coals basting occasionally with marinade: 5 minutes on each side for medium rare; 7 minutes on each side for medium. **Serves 4 to 6.**

TIPS: Large cherry tomatoes, onion, and bell-pepper wedges can be skewered between lamb chunks. Brush with marinade.

To broil kebabs in the oven, preheat oven to Broil and follow instructions above.

If you use wooden skewers soak them in water for about an hour before threading meat; otherwise they may ignite.

BROILED LAMB CHOPS

INGREDIENTS:
1 tablespoon dried basil
1 tablespoon dried marjoram
1 tablespoon dried thyme
12 1-inch-thick rib lamb chops

EQUIPMENT:
Small bowl or 2-cup measuring cup

Thoroughly mix herbs in bowl, then rub mixture on both sides of each chop and chill 1 hour. Broil chops 4 inches from heat for 6 minutes, then turn and cook 4 more minutes for medium rare. **Serves 4 to 6.**

ROAST LEG OF SPRING LAMB
WITH FRESH MINT VINAIGRETTE

For delicious lamb *do not overcook*. The roast is at its juicy, succulent best when served rare or medium rare.

INGREDIENTS:
1 leg of spring lamb, 6 to 7 pounds, trimmed of
   all excess fat
2 garlic cloves, sliced into about 6 slivers each
3 tablespoons extra-virgin olive oil
Salt and freshly ground black pepper to taste
1 or more cups dry white wine
Vinaigrette:
⅔ cup olive oil
¼ cup white wine vinegar
1 teaspoon sugar
Salt and freshly ground black pepper to taste
¾ cup finely chopped fresh mint leaves

EQUIPMENT:
Deep roasting pan with rack
Small (1-quart) mixing bowl

TIP: To shorten cooking time, have the butcher bone and tie leg of lamb. Insert garlic slivers and marinate as indicated above. Preheat oven to 425°. Sear lamb on all sides over high heat in ovenproof skillet; transfer to oven and roast *without basting* 25 to 30 minutes, then proceed with recipe.

With the point of a sharp knife, pierce lamb in as many places as you have garlic slivers. Insert slivers into slits. Refrigerate lamb 2 hours, then remove from refrigerator and let stand at room temperature 30 minutes.

Preheat oven to 325°. Rub leg of lamb all over with oil, sprinkle with salt and pepper, place on rack in roasting pan, and pour 1 cup of the wine around it. Insert meat thermometer in thickest part of meat away from bone and roast 20 minutes per pound for rare (135 to 140° degrees internal temperature) or 25 minutes per pound for medium (150 to 155° internal temperature). Baste occasionally with wine and any juices that accumulate, adding more wine if necessary.

To make vinaigrette, place all ingredients except mint in bowl and whisk until sugar completely dissolves. Add mint and mix well. Cover bowl and let it sit about 30 minutes to allow flavors to blend. Immediately before serving, whisk again.

Transfer lamb to heated platter and let stand about 15 minutes. Slice thinly and serve with vinaigrette. **Serves 8.**

Spring Celebration

Cornelius's Caponata
Green Bean Salad
Festive Baked Ham with Honey-Mustard Glaze
Green Rice
Summer Squash
Poached Pears
Freezer Curried Cookies

"For winter's rains and ruins are over . . .
Blossom by blossom the spring begins."
—Algernon Charles Swinburne

You're thoroughly tired of your winter wardrobe—and your winter menus. It seems you've fed your family casseroles, stews, and thick, hearty soups for months on end, and though they're delicious, everyone's getting a little tired of them, too.

Then, just when you think winter might last forever, it's spring! Celebrate the change of season with a bright and festive holiday meal that will raise the spirits of your family, your guests, and yourself. Tender-crisp green beans, rosy succulent ham, golden summer squash mingled with lush red tomatoes—our menu offers a feast for the eye as well as the palate.

And why not brighten your holiday table even more by bringing the spring indoors? Cluster small pots of blooming hyacinths, tulips, and miniature daffodils in a basket in the middle of the table. Not only will they look and smell quite wonderful, but they'll last much longer than cut flowers.

Festive Baked Ham with *Honey-Mustard Glaze (see p. 85), Green Bean Salad (see p. 25),* and *Cornelius's Caponata (see p. 16).*

VEGETABLES

Although broccoli doesn't suit everybody's palate, it is among the most nutritious of vegetables. Delicious without any additional flavorings, it has twice as much vitamin C as oranges, 800 percent of the U.S.D.A. recommended dietary allowance (RDA) for vitamin A and is an excellent source of vitamins E and K.

One cup of broccoli has three times more calcium than a cup of milk (bok choy has six times more calcium than milk). It's a high-fiber, low-calorie (only fifty calories per cup) treat.

Broccoli is a member of the cabbage family—as are cauliflower, brussels sprouts, and turnips—and all are considered "SuperFoods." Add to that group, spinach, carrots, potatoes (which are treated in a later chapter), squash, fennel, corn . . . The list is long, and we hope you've got the idea.

The favored ways to prepare vegetables are steaming (or boiling) or baking with one or two flavorful herbs or seasonings.

ALL ABOUT COOKING VEGETABLES

Boiling—Submerging vegetables in water or another cooking liquid is a reliable and efficient way to cook them. However, don't cook too long, because overcooking boils away valuable vitamins and nutrients. Because the cooking water after boiling contains some of the nutrients as well as the flavor of the vegetable, it can be a valuable addition to stocks or soups. Once the vegetable is cooled, freeze the liquid for later use. Be sure to label it.

Steaming—cooking *over*, not in, boiling water—is an easy and nutritionally sound method for preparing most fresh vegetables. Because many of the vitamins in fresh vegetables are water soluble, their nutritional value is considerably diminished when boiled; thus steaming assures maximum vitamin retention. To keep their fresh, bright color as well as most of their nutrients, put vegetables in a steaming basket (see p. 97) or colander in a large pot *over* an inch or so of rapidly boiling water. Cover immediately and steam until tender but not mushy.

Baking—Certain vegetables—especially potatoes—taste entirely different when baked. A potato baked unadulterated by cooking accoutrements or seasonings, and without a lick of fanfare, can be the highlight of any meal.

Blanching is used to highlight a vegetable's color, loosen skins for peeling, mellow bitterness, or enhance further cooking. In blanching, vegetables are put in rapidly boiling water for a very short period of time. The trick is to use lots of water—7 quarts for 2 to 3 pounds of vegetables—so that the water returns to a boil quickly after vegetables are added. Unless being served immediately, the vegetables are "refreshed" for several minutes in cold water to stop the cooking process. From there, they can be served as is, for a crisp, colorful crudité, or further cooked by sautéing or baking.

Braising involves cooking vegetables slowly on the stove or in the oven, usually in butter and a cooking liquid such as water or broth. With many dishes, the butter can be eliminated. Vegetables that lend themselves well to braising are carrots, cauliflower, celery, fennel, leeks, and onions.

Broiling and grilling—Most vegetables may be either oven-broiled on skewers or on a rack in a shallow baking pan, or grilled over hot coals. Marinate vegetables or brush with oil and sprinkle with herbs before cooking.

CAUTION: NO TWO VEGETABLES ARE ALIKE

Cooking times given here are only approximate. They can vary—sometimes widely—according to the size, age, and nature of the vegetables. Check at intervals to avoid overcooking. Fully ripe vegetables fresh from a garden cook very rapidly compared with those from the supermarket.

Glazed Carrots, see p. 102.

Artichokes

Preparation: Wash; cut off stems and slice off about 1 inch of tops; trim tips off remaining leaves.
Steam: 30 to 40 minutes, adding more water as it evaporates.
Boil: 35 to 45 minutes in a covered pan, keeping an inch of water in the pan at all times.
Herbs: Basil, chervil, marjoram, oregano, parsley.
Other seasonings: Garlic, ginger, lemon, mustard, vinegar, white wine.
Serving suggestions:
● Serve hot or cold with vinaigrette
● Sauté artichoke hearts in butter or oil with onions and garlic.

Asparagus

Preparation: Wash; cut off tough white ends. Peel any tough or thick stalks with a sharp vegetable peeler, from base to tip.
Steam: Pencil-thin or peeled spears, 7 to 10 minutes; medium to thick spears, 10 to 15 minutes.
Boil: Place asparagus in pan with water just to cover. Bring water to boil, cover and cook thin stalks 5 to 7 minutes, thicker stalks 7 to 10 minutes.
Herbs: Chives, lemon balm, poppy seed, sesame seed.
Other seasonings: Lemon juice, orange juice, soy sauce, vinegar.
Serving suggestions:
● Serve hot with melted butter and fresh lemon juice.
● Serve cold with curried mayonnaise or vinaigrette.

Beans, Green

Preparation: Trim stem ends; leave whole or slice into 1-inch pieces.
Steam: 10 to 15 minutes until crisp-tender.
Boil: 5 to 10 minutes in salted water, uncovered.
Herbs: Chives, dill, marjoram, mint, oregano, thyme, tarragon.
Other seasonings: Garlic, lemon juice, soy sauce, vinegar.
Serving suggestions:
● Serve hot with snipped fresh chives or lemon juice and slivered almonds.
● Sauté with butter, onions, and tomatoes.

Beans, Lima

Preparation: Shell and wash.
Steam: 20 to 25 minutes.
Boil: 12 to 20 minutes.
Herbs: Marjoram, oregano, parsley, savory, tarragon, thyme.
Other seasonings: Lemon juice, vinegar.
Serving suggestions:
● Toss with sour cream and freshly ground black pepper.
● Toss with lemon juice, butter, and parsley.

Beets

Preparation: Wash; trim beet green tops to 1 inch. Do not peel before cooking. When cool enough to handle, slip off skins and trim root and tops.
Steam: Young beets, 40 minutes; older, tougher beets, 1 to 1½ hours.
Boil: Bring enough water to cover to a boil and cook, uncovered, 35 to 40 minutes.
Herbs: Caraway seed, celery seed, chives, dill, mint, thyme.
Other seasonings: Orange juice, vinegar, cloves, cinnamon, ginger.
Serving suggestions:
● Slice and toss with orange juice and grated orange rind.
● Place on a bed of steamed beet greens seasoned to taste with salt and pepper.

Broccoli

Preparation: Wash, remove outer leaves and cut off tough ends of stems; slice thick stems in halves or quarters lengthwise.
Steam: 10 to 12 minutes.
Boil: Cook covered in salted boiling water for 7 to 10 minutes.
Herbs: Lemon balm, sesame seeds, thyme.
Other seasonings: Lemon juice, garlic, orange juice, soy sauce, vinegar, curry powder.
Serving suggestions:
● Sprinkle with lemon juice and pepper.
● Season with pepper and toss with a bit of freshly grated Parmesan cheese.

Brussels Sprouts

Preparation: Wash; remove any discolored outer leaves and trim stems.
Steam: 14 to 18 minutes.
Boil: Cook covered in salted, boiling water 10 to 15 minutes.
Herbs: Basil, caraway seed, parsley, thyme.
Other seasonings: Garlic, mustard seed, vinegar.
Serving suggestions:
● Sprinkle with grated cheese and chopped parsley.
● Shred leaves in food processor; sauté with butter, basil, onion, and thyme.

Cabbage

Preparation: Wash; remove outer leaves, trim core, and cut into wedges.
Steam: 10 to 15 minutes.
Boil: Cook covered in salted boiling water 5 to 8 minutes.
Herbs: Caraway seed, celery seed, dill, juniper berries, mint, mustard seed, savory, marjoram.
Other seasonings: Mustard, cloves, vinegar, white wine, beer.
Serving suggestions:
● Serve with browned butter, salt and pepper to taste.
● Serve with mustard, salt, and pepper.

Carrots

Preparation: Cut off tops and trim ends. Peel thin layer of skin with a vegetable peeler or scrub well. Very small, tender carrots may be cooked whole; cut larger ones into ½-inch rounds or thin strips.
Steam: 20 to 25 minutes, whole; 8 to 12 minutes, slices or strips.
Boil: Cook partially uncovered in boiling water; 15 to 18 minutes, whole; 8 to 12 minutes for slices or strips.
Herbs: Chervil, dill, marjoram, mint, parsley, thyme, savory, tarragon.
Other seasonings: Brown sugar, orange or apple juice, allspice, anise, cardamom, cinnamon, ginger, nutmeg, curry powder, cumin.
Serving suggestions:
● Toss with plain yogurt and a dash of nutmeg.
● Toss with sautéed chopped apples and raisins.

Cauliflower

Preparation: Wash, remove outer leaves, trim core and stem; cut or break into florets, or leave head whole.
Steam: 10 to 15 minutes for florets.
Boil: Place whole head stem-side down in boiling water and cook uncovered 15 to 18 minutes; for florets, boil 8 to 12 minutes.
Herbs: Chives, dill, marjoram, mustard seed, parsley, tarragon.
Other seasonings: Paprika, cumin, curry powder.
Serving suggestions:
● Sprinkle with grated Cheddar cheese or Mornay Sauce (see p. 124).
● Toss with butter, sprinkle with bread crumbs.

Corn on the Cob

Preparation: Remove husks and corn silk; trim stems.
Steam: 5 to 10 minutes.
Boil: Bring water to boil, add corn and cook uncovered 5 to 7 minutes.
Serving suggestion:
● Butter, salt, and pepper; it truly doesn't need anything else.

Corn Kernels

Preparation: Cut corn from the cob with a sharp knife.
Steam: 3 to 5 minutes
Boil: 3 to 5 minutes
Herbs: Chives, cilantro, dill, lemon balm, mint, parsley, thyme.
Other seasonings: Saffron, cumin, paprika.
Serving suggestions:
● Combine with sliced scallions, butter, and a dab of sour cream.
● Combine with finely diced red bell pepper.

Eggplant

Preparation: Wash; peel if skin is tough; trim stem; cut into cubes, or ½-inch rounds or strips; drizzle with lemon juice to remove bitterness.
Steam: 5 to 7 minutes.
Boil: 5 to 9 minutes.
Broil: Drizzle with olive oil and broil 4 to 6 minutes.

Herbs: Basil, chives, marjoram, oregano, parsley, thyme.
Other seasonings: Garlic.
Serving suggestions:
- Serve with diced tomato and onion.
- Sprinkle with shredded mozzarella or fontina cheese.

Greens (beet tops, collards, turnip and mustard greens, spinach, Swiss chard, watercress)

Preparation: Wash and drain leaves thoroughly, more than once if necessary. (To wash, soak in bowl of cold water, swish by hand, drain, and repeat until no sand or grit collects on bottom of bowl.) Remove tough stems. Tear large leaves into smaller pieces.
Steam: 5 to 12 minutes.
Boil: With just the water that remains on leaves after washing, cook 5 to 10 minutes in covered pan.
Seasonings: Lemon or lime juice, garlic, soy sauce, vinegar, onion, paprika.
Serving suggestions:
- Drizzle vinegar over greens, season with salt and pepper.
- Sauté briefly with garlic and a dab of butter.

Onions

Preparation: Trim ends and peel. Cut into quarters, slices, or, if small, leave whole.
Steam: 18 to 22 minutes, depending on size.
Boil: 13 to 17 minutes in just enough water to cover.
Herbs: Caraway seed, cinnamon, cloves, mustard seed, oregano, thyme.
Other seasonings: Curry powder, nutmeg.
Serving suggestions:
- Toss with melted butter, salt and pepper, and a dash of cinnamon or cloves.
- Dice onion; sauté with diced green bell pepper.

Parsnips

Preparation: Wash; trim ends and peel. Leave whole or cut into quarters, 2-inch chunks, or thin strips.
Steam: Quarters or chunks for 10 to 15 minutes; whole for 15 to 20 minutes.
Boil: Quarters or chunks, 8 to 12 minutes; whole, 10 to 20 minutes.
Herbs: Chives, marjoram, parsley.
Other seasonings: Honey, brown sugar, cinnamon, ginger, mace, nutmeg.
Serving suggestions:
- Serve with butter and sautéed chopped apples.
- Puree and season with a dab of butter and a sprinkle of nutmeg.

Peas, Green

Preparation: Shell and wash.
Steam: 5 to 10 minutes.
Boil: 4 to 8 minutes.
Herbs: Basil, dill, marjoram, mint, poppy seed.
Other seasonings: Lemon juice.
Serving suggestions:
- Sprinkle with lemon juice and finely chopped mint leaves.
- Serve with herbed butter.

Peas, Snow

Preparation: Wash and remove tips and strings along sides of pods.
Steam: 3 to 5 minutes.
Boil: 2 to 3 minutes.
Herbs: Basil, caraway seeds, chervil, chives, dill, lemon balm, mint, sesame seeds, thyme.
Other seasonings: Garlic, ginger, soy sauce, sesame oil.
Serving suggestions:
- Toss with sesame oil and toasted sesame seeds.
- Serve cold in salads.

Potatoes

Preparation: Peel if desired; leave whole, cut into quarters, chunks, or slices. Keep covered with cold water until ready to cook.
Steam: Whole, 30 to 35 minutes; quarters, slices, or chunks, 15 to 25 minutes, depending on thickness—test with fork for doneness.
Boil: Whole, 25 to 40 minutes; quarters, slices, or chunks, 10 to 20 minutes, depending on size. Place new potatoes in already-boiling water. Other potatoes are placed in water and brought to a boil.
Bake: Pierce whole baking potatoes with a fork (do not peel). Bake at 400° 40 to 60 minutes.
Herbs: Chives, dill, rosemary, *fines herbes*.
Other seasonings: Garlic, paprika.
Serving suggestions:
- Toss steamed or boiled new potatoes or small red potatoes with butter and dill.
- Serve baked potatoes with pureed cottage cheese and snipped chives.

Rutabagas (Yellow Turnips)

Preparation: Peel and cut into eighths.
Steam: 25 to 35 minutes.
Boil: Cook uncovered in salted, boiling water, 20 to 25 minutes.
Herbs: Dill.
Other seasonings: Cinnamon, nutmeg, brown sugar, maple syrup.
Serving suggestions:
- Mash with melted butter and a pinch of nutmeg.
- Serve with a splash of maple syrup or a sprinkling of brown sugar.

Squash, Summer (yellow and zucchini)

Preparation: Do not peel. Trim ends and cut into ½-inch rounds. (Very small squash may be left whole.)
Steam: 5 to 8 minutes.
Boil: 5 to 8 minutes.
Herbs: Basil, chives, cilantro, dill, mint, fennel seed, marjoram, oregano, parsley, savory, thyme.
Other seasonings: Garlic, lemon juice.
Serving suggestions:
- Sprinkle with finely chopped parsley, fresh lemon juice and thyme.
- Sauté in butter or oil with shallots or garlic.

Vegetables in steamer

Squash, Winter (banana, butternut, Hubbard, buttercup, acorn, spaghetti)

Preparation: Peel and cut into slices or cubes. For baking, leave unpeeled, cut in half and remove seeds.
Steam: 8 to 12 minutes; Hubbard will take twice as long.
Boil: 6 to 9 minutes; twice as long for Hubbard.
Bake: Place squash cut-side up in baking pan. Add ¼ cup water for each half. Cover with foil and bake 25 to 50 minutes, depending on size of squash.
Herbs: Oregano, rosemary, thyme.
Other seasonings: Orange or apple juice, honey, brown sugar, cardamom, cloves, coriander, curry powder, ginger, mace, nutmeg.
Serving suggestions:
● Toss with butter and sprinkle with nutmeg.
● Sprinkle with brown sugar.

Tomatoes

Preparation: Remove stems from cherry tomatoes and leave whole. Other tomatoes can be left whole, sliced or quartered.
Steam: Cherry tomatoes: 1 to 2 minutes.
Boil: Cook sliced tomatoes, using no additional liquid, 5 to 10 minutes over medium heat, covered, and stirring occasionally.
Bake: Whole or halved tomatoes: 15 to 25 minutes, depending on size, at 350°.
Herbs: Bay leaf, basil, chives, cilantro, dill, fennel seed, marjoram, oregano, parsley, rosemary, sage, savory, sesame seed, tarragon, thyme.
Serving suggestions:
● Toss cherry tomatoes with minced fresh basil and a pinch of marjoram.
● Sprinkle baked/steamed tomatoes with freshly grated Parmesan cheese and pepper.

Turnips

Preparation: Cut into quarters—or eighths if very large — and peel.
Steam: 20 to 35 minutes.
Boil: Cook uncovered 10 to 25 minutes in boiling, salted water.
Herbs: Basil, dill, chives, parsley, thyme.
Other seasonings: Brown sugar, pepper.
Serving suggestion:
● Toss with butter, parsley, and pepper.
● Puree with cooked carrots and butter. Sprinkle with snipped chives.

Braised Red Cabbage

BRAISED RED CABBAGE

Delicious hot or cold. The pungent and peppery taste of red cabbage is toned down when braised. An excellent accompaniment to ham, pork, or sausage.

INGREDIENTS:
1 head red cabbage, about 2 pounds, cored and
    thinly sliced
1 apple, cored and chopped
⅓ cup red-wine vinegar
⅓ cup water
4 cloves stuck in ½ onion
1 bay leaf
Salt and freshly ground black pepper to taste

EQUIPMENT:
2½-quart covered casserole

Preheat oven to 325°. Combine all ingredients and bake covered 2 hours, stirring occasionally and adding more water if necessary. Remove onion and bay leaf before serving. **Serves 6.** ● ■

STIR-FRY BOK CHOY

Bok choy, a Chinese cabbage, has a fresher taste than the common variety of cabbage. Serve with Asian Chicken (see p. 55) and rice.

INGREDIENTS:
1 large head bok choy, stem end trimmed
1 tablespoon vegetable or peanut oil
1 large garlic clove, halved
¼ cup julienned daikon radish or sliced water
    chestnuts
Soy sauce

EQUIPMENT:
10-inch skillet or wok

Cut bok choy crosswise into 1- or 2-inch pieces. Heat oil in skillet; add garlic and bok choy. Stir-fry about 3 minutes or until bok choy is wilted. Discard garlic, toss with daikon or water chestnuts, and serve with soy sauce on the side. **Serves 4.** ● ■

Broccoli, Carrot, and Spinach Timbales

BROCCOLI, CARROT, AND SPINACH TIMBALES

Although this elegant vegetable dish takes time, it isn't difficult.

INGREDIENTS:
1 pound carrots, peeled and sliced in discs
1 pound broccoli, trimmed and cut into stems
   with florets
4 eggs
2 tablespoons light cream
Salt and freshly ground black pepper to taste
½ teaspoon dried ground cardamom
½ teaspoon dried ground mace
5 tablespoons butter or margarine
8 cups fresh spinach

EQUIPMENT:
2 2-quart covered saucepans with steamers
Food processor or blender
Small (1-quart) mixing bowl
6 ½-cup timbale molds or ramekins
Large baking pan

Preheat oven to 350°. Steam carrots and broccoli in separate pans for 15 minutes or until very soft. Puree each vegetable separately in food processor. In bowl, whisk together eggs and cream; divide mixture in half and blend with pureed vegetables in separate pans. Add cardamom to carrots and mace to broccoli; add 2 tablespoons of butter to each and cook over low heat for just a minute.

Place broccoli puree in greased ramekins; top with carrot puree. Place ramekins in bain-marie, a large baking pan with hot water that reaches halfway up the ramekins, and bake 20 to 25 minutes or until a toothpick inserted in the center comes out clean. When timbales are nearly done, thoroughly wash spinach and place in saucepan with water still clinging to leaves. Cover and cook over low heat for 2 to 3 minutes. Serve unmolded timbales on a bed of spinach. **Serves 6.**

TIPS: If you don't have mace and cardamom on hand, season the timbales with nutmeg.

To save time, microwave the vegetables.

Broccoli, Carrot, and Spinach Timbales in bain-marie

Broccoli with Lemon-Chive Sauce

BROCCOLI WITH LEMON-CHIVE SAUCE

The sauce is wonderful with broccoli, it's equally delicious served over white fish and many other vegetables. Try it with asparagus and carrots.

INGREDIENTS:
1 pound broccoli, trimmed and cut into stems
    with florets
⅓ cup butter or margarine
3 tablespoons finely chopped fresh chives
1 tablespoon fresh lemon juice
Dash of salt and freshly ground black pepper to
    taste

EQUIPMENT:
2-quart covered saucepan with steamer
Small saucepan

Steam broccoli about 10 minutes until just tender. Melt butter in small saucepan over low heat or in microwave oven. Remove from heat; add chives and lemon juice; blend and pour over broccoli. **Serves 4.**

CAULIFLOWER CURRY

INGREDIENTS:
1 large head cauliflower, cored and cut into small
    florets
3 tablespoons vegetable oil
1 onion, coarsely chopped
1 garlic clove, minced
1 tablespoon curry powder *or*
    1 teaspoon coriander and
    ½ teaspoon ground ginger and
    ¼ teaspoon cumin seeds and
    ¼ teaspoon mustard seeds and
    ½ teaspoon turmeric
Salt to taste

EQUIPMENT:
10-inch skillet

In skillet, heat oil until very hot, add onion and garlic and sauté one minute. Add curry powder or spices and cook 5 minutes, stirring constantly. Add cauliflower, reduce heat to medium, and cook about 20 minutes. Cauliflower should be tender but firm. **Serves 6.**

MICROWAVE TIP: To reduce cooking time, microwave cauliflower in 3 tablespoons water 6 to 8 minutes covered on HIGH. Add cauliflower to spices and cook 5 minutes on stove.

PUREED CAULIFLOWER

Wonderfully satisfying on a cold winter's night. Serve with poultry or fish.

INGREDIENTS:
1 head cauliflower, about 3 pounds, cut in florets
8 tablespoons grated Swiss cheese
1 teaspoon ground nutmeg
2½ cups Béchamel Sauce (see p. 124)
Salt and freshly ground white pepper to taste
3 tablespoons dried bread crumbs

EQUIPMENT:
6-quart stockpot
Food processor or blender
8-inch square baking dish

Preheat oven to 375°. Place florets in boiling water; boil 10 minutes until just tender. Drain well. Transfer to food processor or blender. If you use a blender, puree in batches. Add 6 tablespoons of the cheese and nutmeg. Puree, gradually adding all the Béchamel Sauce. Add salt and pepper to taste and place in buttered baking dish. Top with bread crumbs and remaining Swiss cheese. Bake, loosely covered, 20 minutes. Remove cover and continue to bake 5 to 10 minutes until top is lightly browned. **Serves 6.**

MICROWAVE TIP: Microwave cauliflower in 3 tablespoons water, covered, on HIGH 8 to 10 minutes or until tender. Drain and puree, then finish recipe.

BROILED EGGPLANT

INGREDIENTS:
2 small eggplants, about ½ pound each
2 to 3 tablespoons olive oil
Salt and freshly ground black pepper to taste
1 teaspoon dried oregano
½ teaspoon dried marjoram
¼ cup grated Parmesan cheese (optional)

EQUIPMENT:
3-quart saucepan
Baking sheet

Bring approximately 2 quarts salted water to boil. Trim ends of unpeeled eggplants. Cut each eggplant in half lengthwise, then cut halves into 3 lengthwise slices. Boil, uncovered, 3 to 5 minutes; then refresh under cold running water and pat dry. Brush slices on all sides with olive oil. Sprinkle with salt, pepper, oregano, and marjoram.

Set oven to Broil. Place on baking sheet and broil 2 to 3 minutes. Turn and broil 2 to 3 more minutes. Sprinkle with Parmesan cheese and serve. **Serves 4.**

EGGPLANT is traditionally salted and drained before cooking, a process that takes 30 minutes. This removes the excess water; it also results in the eggplant's absorbing less fat in the cooking process. We prefer blanching in boiling salted water for 5 minutes. It's a time-saver, and the eggplant absorbs even less fat than when salted and drained.

BRAISED FENNEL

INGREDIENTS:
1 large fennel bulb
1 to 2 cups water or chicken broth, canned or
   homemade
Olive oil (optional)
Grated Parmesan, Gruyère, Monterey Jack, or
   Cheddar cheese for garnish (optional)

EQUIPMENT:
10-inch covered skillet or au gratin pan

TIP: You can also serve fennel with a vinaigrette.
For an Italian-style luncheon, serve with salami,
proscuitto, or sausage and marinated vegetables.
Leftover fennel can be refrigerated and warmed
to room temperature for serving. Or chop cooked
fennel and add to a simple green salad.

Cut off some of the feathery fronds of fennel
stalk and reserve for garnish. Trim stalks above fennel
bulb. Trim base of stalk to remove any discolored areas. If outer layer is excessively thick, tough,
or bruised, remove or shave with swivel peeler. Cut
bulbs in half lengthwise through the bottom. Cut
each half into quarters and with paring knife remove
hard core.

Place fennel pieces, flat sides down, in a skillet.
Add enough water or chicken broth to come ¼ of
the way up the bulb. Replenish during cooking if
necessary. Bring to a boil, cover, and simmer until
tender, 10 to 20 minutes depending on thickness.
Turn pieces over once. Fennel should be crisp-
tender, not mushy. Drain and serve, or brush with
olive oil and broil briefly to crisp ends. **Serves 4.**
● ■

GLAZED CARROTS

INGREDIENTS:
8 carrots, peeled and julienned
2 tablespoons melted butter or margarine
1 tablespoon honey
1 tablespoon chopped Italian flat-leaf
   parsley or dill

EQUIPMENT:
2-quart covered ovenproof saucepan or casserole

See photo, p. 90.

Preheat oven to 350°. Place carrots in saucepan
with enough water to cover. Bring to a boil and cook
10 minutes (or steam). Drain off water and mix in
butter and honey. Cover and bake 15 minutes, stirring once. Sprinkle with parsley and/or dill to serve.
Serves 4. ● ■

MICROWAVE DIRECTIONS: Cook carrots in a
microwave-safe dish with 1 tablespoon of water 9
minutes on HIGH. Mix with honey and butter and
microwave on HIGH another 2 minutes. To serve,
garnish as above.

SAUTÉED MUSHROOMS

INGREDIENTS:
¼ cup butter or margarine
1¼ pounds mushrooms, trimmed and sliced
Juice of ¼ lemon
1 tablespoon chopped fresh marjoram leaves or 1
   teaspoon dried marjoram
Salt and freshly ground black pepper to taste

EQUIPMENT:
10-inch sauté pan

Melt butter in sauté pan over medium heat.
Add mushrooms, lemon juice, and marjoram and
sauté gently 15 minutes. Add salt and pepper as
desired. **Serves 4 to 6.**

GARLIC GREEN BEANS AND TOMATO

INGREDIENTS:
1 pound green beans
1 tablespoon olive oil
1 garlic clove, minced
1 tomato, peeled and finely chopped
1 tablespoon white-wine vinegar
Salt and freshly ground black pepper to taste

EQUIPMENT:
2-quart covered saucepan with steamer
8-inch sauté pan

Steam or boil green beans 3 to 5 minutes until crisp-tender. Heat oil in sauté pan over medium-high heat; add garlic and sauté 1 minute. Add remaining ingredients; heat 5 minutes. **Serves 4.**

● ■

Garlic Green Beans and Tomato

BRAISED LEEKS

INGREDIENTS:
8 medium leeks, root end and greens trimmed
3 tablespoons butter or margarine
Salt and freshly ground black pepper to taste
¼ cup fresh or dried bread crumbs
2 tablespoons grated Parmesan cheese

EQUIPMENT:
9 × 13-inch baking dish

Preheat oven to 350°. Place leeks side by side (they can overlap slightly) in baking dish. Add butter and enough water to cover. Bake 45 minutes; check dish frequently and add water and/or butter as necessary. Turn leeks occasionally so that they will brown evenly. Sprinkle with salt and pepper, bread crumbs, and Parmesan cheese and cook 5 to 15 more minutes until leeks are lightly browned and easily pierced with a knife. **Serves 4.**

LEEKS require careful cleaning. Wash leeks to remove grit. Trim leaf ends, leaving about 3 to 4 inches of green tops. Trim root ends and cut an X in the base of each. Soak again in water and wash carefully under running water, spreading leaves to remove all sand.

CORN PUDDING

Wonderful with grilled meats, chops, sausage. Fresh summer corn
needs no extra seasoning.

INGREDIENTS:
2 eggs, separated
6 ears corn, grated
1 tablespoon melted butter or margarine
1 tablespoon sugar
½ cup milk
½ teaspoon baking powder
Salt and freshly ground black pepper to taste
Pinch of nutmeg (optional)

EQUIPMENT:
2 medium (2½ quart) mixing bowls
2½-quart casserole or souffle dish
Electric mixer

Preheat oven to 350°. Beat egg yolks lightly
and egg whites until stiff. Mix all ingredients except
egg whites. Fold in beaten egg whites and pour into
baking dish. Bake 30 minutes or until knife inserted
in center comes out clean. **Serves 4 to 6.**

TIP: Corn *must* be grated. You can use frozen corn-
on-the-cob, but not frozen kernels.

BAKED ONIONS

Do as the Italians do and serve these onions at room temperature
as part of an antipasto assortment.

INGREDIENTS:
4 large yellow onions, unpeeled and left whole
2 tablespoons water
2 tablespoons plus 2 teaspoons butter or
    margarine
2 garlic cloves, minced
1 tablespoon olive oil
½ cup bread crumbs, fresh or dried
4 tablespoons grated Parmesan cheese
Salt and freshly ground black pepper to taste
¼ teaspoon dried marjoram
¼ teaspoon dried oregano
½ teaspoon dried thyme
Pinch cayenne pepper

EQUIPMENT:
1½-quart covered shallow casserole
8-inch sauté pan
Medium (2½-quart) mixing bowl

Preheat oven to 350°. Put onions in baking dish
with water. Cover and bake 20 minutes or until
onions are barely tender. Remove from oven and
when onions are cool enough to handle, slip off
skins. Cut off tops and hollow onions out, reserving
the insides and leaving a ½-inch-thick shell. Discard
any liquid that remains in baking dish and grease
with 2 teaspoons butter. Place onions upright in
baking dish.

Raise oven temperature to 400°. Coarsely chop
reserved onion. Heat oil in sauté pan over medium-
high heat. Add garlic and sauté 2 minutes. Combine
with onion pulp in bowl. Add bread crumbs, cheese,
salt, and pepper and stuff onion shells with the
mixture. Melt 2 tablespoons of the butter, mix with
herbs and cayenne and pour over stuffed onions.
Cover and bake 20 minutes. Remove cover, baste
with pan juices, and bake 10 more minutes, or until
stuffing is lightly browned on top. **Serves 4.**

TIP: Olive oil can easily be used instead of butter
to cut down on cholesterol.

MICROWAVE TIP: To shorten cooking time, microwave the onions for 8 to 10 minutes, then stuff
and bake as above.

Corn Pudding

Red Onion Preserves

RED ONION PRESERVES

Serve as a condiment with ground beef dishes—or serve on the side with beef, poultry, or fish.

INGREDIENTS:
¼ cup olive oil
1 tablespoon minced garlic
½ teaspoon ground cumin
½ teaspoon red pepper flakes
1 teaspoon dried oregano
1 bay leaf
¼ cup balsamic vinegar
Salt to taste
1 teaspoon coarsely ground black pepper
3 pounds red onions, cut in ½-inch slices

EQUIPMENT:
12-inch covered sauté pan or sautôir

Heat oil in sauté pan over medium-high heat. Add garlic and sauté 1 minute. Add remaining ingredients, except onions, and stir. Add onion, stir, and reduce heat to low. Cover and cook about 45 minutes to 1 hour until onion is very soft, stirring several times. Do not allow to burn. Let cool to room temperature and refrigerate at least 1 day. To serve, remove bay leaf and let preserves return to room temperature. **Yield: about 2 cups.** ● ■

MICROWAVE DIRECTIONS: Combine all ingredients except salt, pepper, and vinegar in shallow microwave dish. Loosely cover with glass cover (or microwaveable plastic wrap, but make sure it doesn't touch food.) Cook on HIGH 4 minutes. Stir; cook on HIGH an additional 4 minutes. Add vinegar; continue cooking, uncovered, on HIGH 4 minutes. Add salt and pepper.

Summer Squash

SUMMER SQUASH

INGREDIENTS:
2 tablespoons olive oil
2 medium yellow onions, thinly sliced
2 garlic cloves, minced
6 small summer squash, sliced in ½-inch-thick
   rounds
3 large fresh tomatoes, cored and cut into eighths
¾ cup water
5 fresh basil leaves, finely chopped
Salt and freshly ground black pepper to taste

EQUIPMENT:
2-quart covered saucepan

Heat oil in saucepan over medium heat. Add onion and garlic and sauté 2 to 3 minutes, or until onion is wilted but not brown. Add squash, tomatoes, water, basil, salt, and pepper. Cover pan and cook approximately 10 minutes, or until squash is tender. **Serves 6.** ● ■

BAKED WINTER SQUASH

INGREDIENTS:
3 acorn or butternut squash
¼ cup butter or margarine, melted
2 tablespoons brown sugar
¼ teaspoon grated nutmeg
Pinch of salt
¼ cup fresh orange juice (optional)

EQUIPMENT:
9 × 13-inch baking dish

Preheat oven to 400°. Cut acorn squash in half horizontally or butternut squash in half vertically. Remove seeds. Place skin-side down in baking dish. Brush flesh with melted butter; sprinkle with orange juice, brown sugar, nutmeg, and salt. Add just enough water to cover bottom of baking pan. Cover pan loosely with a tent of aluminum foil and bake 30 minutes. Reduce heat to 350°; remove foil, and continue baking until squash is tender—about 20 more minutes. **Serves 6.**

MICROWAVE DIRECTIONS: Cut squash as directed above. Add all remaining ingredients, except salt, to cavity. Arrange in shallow baking pan, cover with waxed paper and cook on HIGH about 6 minutes or until squash is tender. Rotate dish about halfway through cooking. Allow 3 to 4 minutes of standing time to complete cooking. Add salt to taste.

Zucchini Pancakes

ZUCCHINI PANCAKES

A nice side dish for broiled, grilled, or roasted meats or poultry. It
goes equally well with omelets.

INGREDIENTS:

2 zucchini, about ½ pound each, grated
2 eggs, beaten
2 tablespoons mayonnaise
2 tablespoons finely chopped onion
¼ cup grated Parmesan cheese
¼ cup flour
½ teaspoon chopped fresh oregano leaves or ¼
　teaspoon dried oregano
Salt and freshly ground black pepper to taste
4 tablespoons butter or margarine

EQUIPMENT:

Medium (2½-quart) mixing bowl
10-inch skillet, preferably nonstick, or griddle

Squeeze excess moisture from grated zucchini
by wringing it in paper towels or a clean tea towel
that hasn't been bleached. Combine all ingredients,
except butter, in bowl and mix well. Melt 2 tablespoons of butter or margarine in skillet. Ladle batter
into skillet to make silver-dollar-sized pancakes, or
larger if you prefer. When nicely browned on one
side, flip pancakes over and brown other side. Keep
pancakes on plate in warm oven until all batter is
used. Serve plain or with applesauce or Marinara
Sauce (see p. 123), if desired. **Serves 4 to 6.**

ZUCCHINI PARMESAN

INGREDIENTS:
1 tablespoon olive oil
1 tablespoon butter or margarine
½ small onion or 3 to 4 shallots, finely chopped
3 zucchini, about 1 pound, sliced
½ teaspoon dried oregano or marjoram
Salt and freshly ground black pepper to taste
¼ cup grated Parmesan or Romano cheese

EQUIPMENT:
10-inch sauté pan

In sauté pan, heat olive oil and butter. Sauté onion or shallots about 3 minutes or until wilted. Add zucchini and cook, stirring frequently, about 4 minutes until barely tender. Add lemon juice, oregano, salt, and pepper. Serve garnished with cheese. **Serves 4.**

RATATOUILLE

An excellent side dish or omelet or quiche filling.

INGREDIENTS:
4 tablespoons olive oil
2 medium eggplants, cut into 1-inch-thick rounds and halved (see box, p. 101)
2 medium zucchini or summer squash, cut in 1-inch-thick rounds
1 large red onion, sliced
2 red, green, or yellow bell peppers, cored, seeded, and sliced in 1-inch-thick strips
2 tomatoes, peeled and cubed
2 to 3 garlic cloves, mashed
½ cup chopped fresh basil leaves

See photo, p. iv.

EQUIPMENT:
4½-quart covered Dutch oven

Heat 2 tablespoons oil in saucepan on medium-high heat; add eggplant and zucchini and cook 2 to 3 minutes, stirring occasionally. Add remaining oil, onions, and peppers, reduce heat to medium, and cook 10 more minutes. Add tomatoes and garlic; reduce heat to low, cover, and cook 15 more minutes. Uncover, raise temperature to medium-high, add basil, and cook an additional 15 minutes. Serve warm, at room temperature, or chilled. **Serves 6 to 8.** ● ■ ▼

SAUTÉED GREEN TOMATOES

This Pennsylvania Dutch recipe is deliciously simple and simply delicious!

INGREDIENTS:
¼ cup all-purpose flour
3 tablespoons brown sugar
Salt and freshly ground black pepper to taste
3 or 4 medium-sized green tomatoes, cored and cut crosswise into ½-inch-thick slices
3 or more tablespoons vegetable oil
2 teaspoons finely chopped parsley for garnish

EQUIPMENT:
Pie plate
12-inch sauté pan or sautôir

Combine flour, sugar, salt, and pepper in pie plate and dip tomato slices into mixture, coating both sides. Heat oil in sauté pan over medium heat and sauté tomatoes, a few at a time, about 2 minutes to a side, or until golden brown. Add more oil as necessary. As they are done, place tomatoes on a paper towel on a warm platter. Transfer to serving platter and sprinkle with chopped parsley. **Serves 4.**

TIP: Green tomatoes *are* tomatoes that haven't ripened. They're supposed to be firm.

Zucchini Parmesan

Baked Tomatoes Provençale

BAKED TOMATOES PROVENÇALE

Wonderful when made with plump, luscious, vine-ripened tomatoes; not so wonderful if the tomatoes are the pallid supermarket variety. The herbs must be fresh, too—we don't recommend substituting dried ones in this recipe.

INGREDIENTS:

2 garlic cloves, minced
1 shallot, minced
2 tablespoons finely chopped fresh Italian flat-leaf
 parsley
2 tablespoons finely chopped fresh basil leaves
1 teaspoon finely chopped fresh thyme leaves
Salt and coarsely ground black pepper to taste
3 tablespoons, plus 1 teaspoon olive oil
4 large, ripe tomatoes, cut in half crosswise

EQUIPMENT:

Small (1-quart) mixing bowl
9 × 13-inch baking dish

Preheat oven to 425°. Place garlic, shallot, herbs, salt and pepper, and 3 tablespoons of the oil in bowl and mash to a coarse paste with the back of a wooden spoon. Grease baking dish with remaining oil. Place tomato halves in dish, cut-side up, and spread with herb mixture. Bake 10 minutes, or until topping begins to bubble. Serve hot or at room temperature. **Serves 4.**

Winter Vegetable Potpourri

WINTER VEGETABLE POTPOURRI

INGREDIENTS:

1 large Idaho potato, peeled
2 medium white turnips, peeled and stem end
  trimmed
12 baby carrots, peeled, or 6 medium carrots,
  peeled and cut in 1-inch-thick rounds
12 small white onions, peeled
¼ pound green beans, cut into 2-inch pieces
3 tablespoons butter or margarine
1 shallot, finely chopped
Salt and freshly ground black pepper to taste
1½ teaspoons fresh thyme leaves or ½ teaspoon
  dried thyme

EQUIPMENT:

3-quart saucepan
10-inch sauté pan

Cut potato and turnips in half, then slice halves into 6 or 8 pieces. Place carrots and onions in saucepan. Add water to cover and a pinch of salt. Bring to a boil over medium heat, then lower heat and simmer 5 minutes. Add turnips and potato and cook 5 minutes. Add green beans; cook 5 more minutes or until just tender. Drain and set aside.

Heat butter in sauté pan over medium heat until bubbling but not brown. Add shallots and cook 2 to 3 minutes. Add drained vegetables, salt, pepper, and thyme. Cook 2 minutes, stirring constantly. **Serves 4.** ● ■ ▼

TIP: To peel small white onions: Drop into boiling water; boil 1 minute; drain under cold running water; trim off both ends; slip off skins.

Vegetable Medley

VEGETABLE MEDLEY

This colorful combination of fresh, luscious vegetables is incredibly versatile. Served piping hot, it makes a hearty one-dish meal for a cold winter day; at room temperature, it's a delicious side dish for a party buffet or a summer picnic.

INGREDIENTS:
¼ cup corn oil
4 large garlic cloves, minced
2 medium leeks, whites and 1 inch of greens, cut into ½-inch rounds
4 medium carrots, peeled and cut into rounds
6 small red new potatoes, scrubbed and cut in half
4 cups chicken or vegetable broth, canned or homemade
4 small zucchini, cut into 1-inch rounds
3 small summer squash, cut into 1-inch rounds
¾ pound green beans
8 plum tomatoes, peeled and quartered
½ cup coarsely chopped fresh parsley
6 fresh basil leaves, coarsely chopped
2 tablespoons minced fresh tarragon leaves, or 1½ teaspoons dried tarragon
Salt and freshly ground black pepper to taste

EQUIPMENT:
6-quart covered stockpot

Heat oil in stockpot over medium heat. Add garlic and leeks. Cook, stirring constantly, 2 to 3 minutes until just wilted. Add carrots and potatoes; gradually pour chicken broth over vegetables. Cover and cook 10 to 12 minutes. Add zucchini, summer squash, and green beans; cook, covered, 10 minutes. Add tomatoes, parsley, basil, tarragon, salt, and pepper, stirring gently to blend. Cover and cook 5 minutes more. Serve hot or at room temperature. **Serves 6 as a main dish, 10 to 12 as a side dish.** ● ■

COCKTAIL PARTY

Cornelius's Caponata
Ginger-Lime Vinaigrette, Curry Dip, and Yogurt Aioli with Crudités
Herbed Yogurt Cheese with Crackers
Herbed Olives
Cocktail Chicken Wings
Party Pecans
Suggested cheeses: gaperone or corolle with pear slices, and/or a brie or chevre

Yogurt Cheese Dip, *Party Pecans*, and *Ginger-Lime Vinaigrette with Crudités*

It's easy to accommodate everyone's taste when serving large groups of people, by choosing foods with a variety of flavors ranging from sweet to spicy. It can be tough to gauge your guests' appetites. Maybe they skipped lunch, or plan to eat your hors d'oeuvres instead of dinner, so it's always best to make more than you think you'll need. (We give you some tips about what to do with any leftovers.) A good rule of thumb is to purchase ¼ pound of vegetables for crudités and two ounces of cheese per person.

Cornelius's Caponata (see p. 16) should be served at room temperature, but can be made a day or two ahead of time. Divide the *Caponata* into several small glass bowls and place strategically on a buffet table next to baskets of bread or crackers. Be sure to include several serving spoons.

Ginger-Lime Vinaigrette (see p. 13), *Curry Dip* (see p. 14), and *Yogurt Aioli* (see p. 16) can be served with vegetables of your choice: Consider cold artichokes or asparagus, zucchini rounds or strips, daikon slices, carrot strips, and snow peas. You might also serve shrimp with the vinaigrette. Prepare the raw vegetables in the morning. Place in tightly-sealed plastic bags and refrigerate.

Herbed Yogurt Cheese (see p. 21) can be prepared a day or two ahead of time. *Herbed Olives* (see p. 14) and *Party Pecans* (see p. 19) can be prepared several days ahead.

Serve *Cocktail Chicken Wings* (see p. 14) on large platters with a lot of cocktail napkins close by.

DON'T THROW OUT THE LEFTOVERS
- Add the crudités to soups or sauté them for lunch.
- Use the *Caponata* in a breakfast omelet.
- Leftover *Ginger-Lime Vinaigrette* makes an excellent marinade for fish.

4TH OF JULY PICNIC

Gazpacho
Minted Cucumber
Sunflower Slaw
Light and Creamy Potato Salad
Fresh Sliced Tomatoes with Fresh Basil and Lemon Juice
Scandinavian Chicken Loaf with Bread or Crackers
Spicy Oven-Fried Chicken
Strawberry Tart
Old-Fashioned Strawberry Lemonade

*Minted Cucumber,
Light and Creamy Potato
Salad,* and *Scandinavian
Chicken Loaf* sandwich

Our "traditional" American menu has been updated for the '90s to remove excess fat. *Minted Cucumbers* (see p. 25) are fat free. *Gazpacho* (see p. 39) can be prepared with or without oil. We've replaced most of the mayonnaise in the *Sunflower Slaw* (see p. 27) with yogurt and in the *Light and Creamy Potato Salad* (see p. 26) with low-fat cottage cheese and yogurt. These substitutions not only reduce the fat but add a delicious new flavor.

Scandinavian Chicken Loaf (see p. 51) is versatile and can be served either in sandwiches—it's delicious with rye bread and honey mustard--or like a country paté to be spread on crackers or French bread. This tasty chicken loaf gets many raves, so make enough for second helpings for everyone. *Spicy Oven Fried Chicken* (see p. 50) satisfies the traditionalists in your crowd. And *Strawberry Tart* (see p. 159) is the perfect ending to a memorable feast.

July 4th wouldn't be complete without lemonade and this is one occasion to take the time to make it the old-fashioned way, with a special Independence Day touch—strawberries.

OLD-FASHIONED STRAWBERRY LEMONADE

INGREDIENTS:
2 quarts water
1 to 1½ cups sugar, depending on how sweet
  you like it
¾ cup freshly squeezed lemon juice
1 pint strawberries, washed and hulled
Mint leaves for garnish

EQUIPMENT:
3-quart saucepan

Boil sugar and water for 3 to 4 minutes to dissolve all the sugar. Chill completely and add lemon juice.

Puree half the strawberries and add to lemonade. Stir well—you'll need to shake or stir occasionally as strawberries will settle. Slice remaining strawberries. Serve lemonade ice cold and garnish with sliced berries and fresh mint. **Yield: 2½ quarts**

BEANS, RICE, POTATOES, AND PASTA

Legumes, rice, potatoes, and pasta are all on nutrition's A-list. Parents, athletes, and dieters love them not only because they taste good but also for the vitamins and minerals, complex carbohydrates, fiber, and protein that they contain.

A BIT OF BEANERY

Dried legumes (beans and peas) are an excellent source of protein, but they are often neglected by cooks who think they require a long soaking and cooking time. Some varieties of legumes do need to be soaked before cooking, but not for endless hours as most people believe, and lentils and split peas require no soaking at all. You can also find many varieties of canned, cooked beans in the supermarket. These are convenient when you're in a hurry, and they have the same flavor and only slightly less nutritional value than those that you cook yourself.

Depending on how much time you have available, prepare legumes in one of the following ways. Whichever method you decide to use, always pick over the dried beans first, removing any foreign matter. Rinse and drain.

To Soak (Traditional Method): Place beans in large pot with three times their volume in water and soak for 8 hours or overnight. (To prevent fermentation, when soaking for more than 12 hours, place pot in refrigerator.)

To Speed-Soak: Place beans in large pot. For each ½ pound of dried beans, add 3 to 4 cups cold water. Bring to a boil, boil 2 minutes, then remove from heat. Cover and let stand 1 hour.

To Cook: Whenever possible, cook in the soaking liquid to retain full nutrients and flavor. Consult the chart below for cooking times, which are based on ½ pound of beans or peas. Cooking times will vary somewhat if you use a larger or smaller quantity.

Don't forget to add beans and peas to soups, stews, casseroles, and grain and vegetable dishes, but they are also delicious on their own. A good way to "disguise" beans for those who don't like them is to cook them separately, puree, then add to soups or stews before serving. Garlic and onions are excellent flavorings for all varieties of legumes; bay leaf, cilantro, cumin, and thyme also enhance their flavor.

	Soak	Cooking Time (Hours)	Uses
Black beans	Yes	1½ to 2	Soups, salads, Mexican and Latin American foods
Black-eyed Peas	Yes	1	Alone, salads
Fava beans	Yes	2½	Purees, soups
Garbanzos (Chick peas)	Yes	2½	Soups, salads, curries, pâtés, pastas, purees
Kidney beans, red, or white, cannellini	Yes	1½ to 2	Chili, stews, soups, salads

asta with arlic, Capers, nd Herbs, e p. 126.

115

	Soak	Cooking Time (Hours)	Uses
Lentils	No	25 minutes	Soups, stews, salads, with grains and vegetables
Lima beans	Yes	1½	Soups, stews, casseroles
Navy beans and small white beans	Yes	1½ to 2	Soups, stews, salads, purees
Pinto beans	Yes	2	Stews, in Mexican dishes
Red beans	Yes	2	With rice, soups, stews, salads
Soybeans	Yes	3 to 4	Casseroles, pâtés, stews
Split peas, Green or yellow	No	45 minutes	Soups

RICE AND POTATOES

If your acquaintance with rice has been limited to the long-grain white variety, it's time to expand your horizons. Basically there are two types of rice: *long-grained*, which cooks up fluffy and dry with grains separate; and *short-grained*, a plump, fat kernel that cooks up creamy, soft, and sticky. Today's cook can choose from a wide range of rice of both kinds: long-grained basmati from India and Pakistan; the short-grained Italian arborio, ideal for risottos; unpolished brown rice; short-grained Oriental rice; even wild rice, which isn't a rice at all but the seed of a North American grass. Each has its own distinctive flavor and texture. And even the most exotic rices can generally be found in any well-stocked supermarket or grocery store.

Most of the potato's vitamins and minerals are found in its skin, which is why in recent years cooks have begun adapting recipes to cook potatoes with the skins on. Today, a wide variety of potatoes can be found in supermarkets and on vegetable stands; we suggest that you try them all and enjoy the subtle differences in flavor and texture.

PASTA, PLEASE

Pasta is easy to cook—and fast. Once you've started preparing pasta dishes, you'll quickly learn how simple it is to adapt recipes and invent your own sauces. Pasta comes in many sizes and shapes and can serve as a first course, side dish, or a meal in itself. Most types are easily reheated and can be prepared in small portions, making it an ideal food for singles and couples. We love fresh pasta, but the dried variety found in boxes on grocery-store shelves is equally good, though it has a slightly different taste.

Keep a box of dried pasta in the pantry, a simple tomato sauce in the freezer, cream or fresh vegetables in the refrigerator, and you'll always have the makings of a delicious meal at hand.

To Cook: Cooking times for pasta vary from 2 to 15 minutes, depending on the variety and whether it is fresh or dried; follow the package directions. Because of the large quantity of water needed, the microwave does not save time when cooking pasta.

You'll need one gallon of water for every pound of pasta; you do not need to add oil. For flavor, add a pinch of salt to the water just before you add pasta. Stir occasionally to prevent sticking. Drain in a colander (you shouldn't rinse with cool water as many of our mothers did) and serve immediately.

To Reheat: Pasta can be reheated in a microwave, at 20- to 30-second intervals on HIGH, or in a 350° to 375° oven, for 15 to 25 minutes.

Serving Sizes: Four ounces of dried pasta yields 2 to 3 cups when cooked, depending on the type of pasta.

The difference between freshly grated Parmesan cheese and the packaged variety is vast. Since Parmesan will keep for a long time in the refrigerator, and can be grated as needed, there's no excuse to use anything but. And by the way, 1 tablespoon of grated Parmesan (all you need for one serving) contains only 25 calories and 2 grams of fat.

WHITE BEAN PUREE

INGREDIENTS:
1 pound dried white navy beans, rinsed and soaked
1 carrot, scrubbed
1 onion, peeled
1 bouquet garni
¼ cup butter or margarine
½ cup light cream
Salt and freshly ground white pepper to taste
Chopped fresh chives for garnish

EQUIPMENT:
6-quart stockpot
Food processor or blender
3-quart saucepan

In stockpot, bring beans, carrot, onion, and bouquet garni to a boil in enough cold water to cover, and simmer for 1½ to 2 hours or until beans are tender. Drain, remove bouquet garni, carrot, and onion and place beans in food processor and puree. Place in saucepan over low heat; add butter and cream and blend. Heat until warmed through; garnish with chives and serve immediately. **Serves 6.**

TIP: A traditional bouquet garni is composed of 2 to 3 parsley sprigs, 2 sprigs of thyme, and a small bay leaf. These are tied together with string or tied in a cheesecloth. You can also place them—plus 4 or 5 whole black peppercorns—in a stainless-steel tea ball. It's easy to find and easy to remove.

BEAN POT

INGREDIENTS:
4 cups large dried lima beans, rinsed and soaked
5 tablespoons butter or margarine
2 medium onions, sliced
1 medium green bell pepper, cored, seeded, and diced
½ cup catsup
½ cup molasses
2 teaspoons dry mustard
½ teaspoon Tabasco sauce
¼ cup cider vinegar
1 to 3 cups diced cooked ham

EQUIPMENT:
6-quart stockpot
10-inch sauté pan
Medium (2½-quart) mixing bowl
4-quart casserole or bean pot

Put lima beans in 2 quarts of boiling water and simmer, covered, about 1 hour or until tender. Add more boiling water if necessary. When limas are tender, drain, reserving 1½ cups of liquid.

Heat oven to 325°. In sauté pan, melt 2 tablespoons of the butter and sauté onions and peppers 2 to 3 minutes until tender-crisp. In mixing bowl, combine catsup, molasses, mustard, Tabasco, vinegar, and the reserved cooking liquid. In casserole, arrange limas, onions and peppers, and ham in layers. Pour catsup mixture over all, dot with remaining 3 tablespoons butter, and bake uncovered 1½ hours. **Serves 10 to 12.**

LENTILS WITH FETA

This dish, as versatile as it is nutritious, can be served hot, cold, or at room temperature. Whichever way you choose, it's delicious!

INGREDIENTS:
1½ cups dried lentils, rinsed
3½ cups water
2 garlic cloves, minced
1 tablespoon chopped fresh thyme leaves, or 1 teaspoon dried thyme
1 bay leaf
¼ teaspoon ground cloves
3 medium-sized carrots, scrubbed or peeled and coarsely chopped
3 medium-sized red onions, coarsely chopped
2 small red, green, or yellow bell peppers, cored, seeded, and finely chopped
¼ cup balsamic vinegar
Salt and freshly ground white pepper to taste
4 tablespoons chopped fresh cilantro leaves, (or parsley, if cilantro is not available)
4 ounces feta cheese, crumbled

EQUIPMENT:
4-quart covered saucepan

In saucepan, combine lentils, water, garlic, thyme, bay leaf, cloves, carrots, and all but ⅓ cup of the onion. Bring to a boil over high heat. Reduce heat, cover, and simmer about 15 minutes, or until lentils are just tender. Remove from heat and discard bay leaf. Add remaining onion, peppers, and vinegar; season to taste with salt and pepper, mix well, and sprinkle with cilantro and feta cheese. **Serves 4 to 6.** ▼ ● ■

TIP: Lentils and vegetables can be simmered, then refrigerated. When ready to serve, simply add remaining onion, peppers and vinegar, seasonings, and feta and reheat if desired.

ORIENTAL RICE

INGREDIENTS:
1 teaspoon minced or grated fresh ginger
1 large garlic clove, minced
2 cups chicken broth, canned or homemade
1½ tablespoons soy sauce
1 cup long-grain white rice
1 cup chopped bok choy or watercress
½ cup sliced water chestnuts
1 teaspoon toasted sesame seeds
4 scallions, white and tender greens, chopped

EQUIPMENT:
2-quart covered saucepan

Combine ginger, garlic, chicken broth, and soy sauce in saucepan. Bring to a boil, then add rice; layer bok choy and water chestnuts on top. Reduce heat, cover, and simmer for 17 minutes or until all liquid is absorbed. Add sesame seeds and scallions; fluff with a fork to mix vegetables. Serve with extra soy sauce on the side. **Serves 4.** ● ■

Oriental Rice

Lentils with Feta

Red Beans and Rice

RED BEANS AND RICE

This dish is a Central and South American cooking staple—and is often found on the breakfast table!

INGREDIENTS:
3 tablespoons vegetable or olive oil
3 small onions, coarsely chopped
2 medium tomatoes, coarsely chopped
2 green bell peppers, cored, seeded, and coarsely chopped
6 garlic cloves, minced
3 tablespoons soy sauce
3 tablespoons Worcestershire sauce
1 tablespoon tomato paste
2 beef bouillon cubes
1 tablespoon dried oregano
2 cans pink beans or kidney beans, drained
Freshly ground black pepper to taste
4 cups water
2 cups long-grain white rice

EQUIPMENT:
3-quart saucepan
3-quart covered saucepan

Heat oil over medium-high heat in saucepan; sauté onions, tomatoes, peppers, and garlic until soft, about 5 minutes. Add soy sauce, Worcestershire, tomato paste, bouillon, and oregano. Mix well, lower heat and simmer 5 to 10 minutes. Add beans, mix well, and simmer at least 15 minutes, stirring occasionally. Add pepper to taste.

While beans are simmering, prepare rice. Bring 4 cups water to a boil. Add rice, stir, lower heat, cover, and cook 15 to 17 minutes or until all the water is absorbed. Fluff with fork before serving. To serve, fill bowls half full with rice and ladle beans over rice. **Serves 6.** ● ■

TIP: If you like this kind of dish on the saucier side, simmer the beans with the saucepan covered.

Green Rice

INGREDIENTS:
4 tablespoons extra-virgin olive oil
2 leeks, white and tender green parts, chopped
1½ cups chicken broth, canned or homemade
1½ cups water
1½ cups long-grain white rice
4 cups finely chopped spinach
¼ cup finely chopped fresh cilantro leaves
½ cup finely chopped watercress

EQUIPMENT:
3-quart covered saucepan

Heat oil in saucepan over medium-high heat; add leeks and sauté 5 to 7 minutes or until soft. Add chicken broth, water, and rice. Stir once, increase heat to high, and bring to a boil. Reduce heat; add spinach, cilantro, and watercress, stir once, cover, and simmer 20 minutes or until all liquid is absorbed. Remove from heat and let stand 5 minutes before serving. **Serves 6.**

Double-Wild Rice

Wild rice has more protein than either white or brown rice and 40 percent fewer calories. If you can't find basmati and arborio where you shop, substitute brown rice and cook according to package directions.

INGREDIENTS:
½ cup wild rice, washed and drained
½ cup basmati or arborio rice
4 cups water
Pinch of salt
1 tablespoon butter or margarine
½ pound wild mushrooms, shiitake, cremini, or portobello, quartered (you can also use "common" mushrooms)
2 tablespoons fresh lemon juice
½ teaspoon dried thyme
Salt and freshly ground black pepper to taste

EQUIPMENT:
2 1-quart covered saucepans
8-inch sauté pan

In each saucepan, bring 2 cups of water and pinch of salt to a rolling boil over high heat. Add wild rice to one saucepan and basmati or arborio rice to the other. Boil 1 minute uncovered, then lower heat, cover, and simmer until water is absorbed and rice is tender. Wild rice will take 45 to 50 minutes; basmati or arborio will take 15 to 20 minutes.

Melt butter in sauté pan over medium heat and sauté mushrooms until tender, about 3 to 5 minutes. Combine rices and mushrooms in serving dish; mix well. Add lemon juice, thyme, salt and pepper, and mix again. **Serves 4 to 6.** ● ■

See photo, p. 59.

Garlic and Herb Mashed Potatoes

INGREDIENTS:
6 large Idaho, Yukon Gold, or all-purpose potatoes, scrubbed, unpeeled and cut in eighths
½ cup (1 stick) butter or margarine
6 garlic cloves, minced
¾ cup milk, half-and-half, or cream
¼ cup chopped scallions, fresh cilantro leaves, or fresh Italian flat-leaf parsley

EQUIPMENT:
4-quart saucepan
8-inch sauté pan
1-quart saucepan
Large (4-quart) mixing bowl
Electric mixer

Put potatoes in large saucepan with enough water to cover and cook 12 to 15 minutes or until tender. Do not overcook. When potatoes are about half cooked, melt butter in sauté pan over medium-high heat; add garlic and sauté 1 minute. Do not let garlic brown. Remove butter and garlic from heat. Warm milk in small saucepan.

Drain potatoes, put them in mixing bowl, and mash coarsely on low speed with an electric mixer, gradually adding melted garlic butter and warm milk. Potatoes should be lumpy, not smooth. Blend in most of the chopped scallions or herbs until thoroughly combined. Transfer to a serving dish and garnish with remaining scallions or herbs. **Serves 6.**

Green Rice

Neapolitan Potatoes

NEAPOLITAN POTATOES

Serve with grilled meats, poultry, tuna, or swordfish.

INGREDIENTS:
½ cup shredded fresh basil leaves
¼ cup chopped fresh Italian flat-leaf parsley
2 teaspoons chopped fresh oregano leaves or ½ teaspoon dried oregano
3 garlic cloves, minced
1½ teaspoons salt
1 teaspoon freshly ground black pepper
½ cup grated Parmesan cheese
½ cup olive oil
6 cups, about 4 pounds, red potatoes, scrubbed, unpeeled, and thinly sliced
2 cups drained and chopped canned tomatoes

EQUIPMENT:
Small (1½-quart) mixing bowl
3-quart covered casserole

Preheat oven to 350°. In bowl, combine basil, parsley, oregano, garlic, salt, pepper, and cheese. Brush casserole with some of the oil. Place one-third of potatoes in casserole; add one-third of tomatoes and drizzle with one-third of remaining oil. Spread one-third of herb mixture on top. Repeat layering twice more. Cover and bake 35 to 40 minutes or until potatoes are tender. Let stand covered 10 to 15 minutes before serving. **Serves 6.**

MICROWAVE TIP: You can make this dish ahead of time and reheat in microwave for 5 to 6 minutes or until thoroughly heated. Or cook this dish in the microwave. It will take about 15 minutes on HIGH, rotating the dish a quarter turn every 5 minutes. Place under the broiler to crisp the top.

Note: Use only a microwaveable glass/ceramic casserole when cooking in both microwave and broiler.

BOILING POTATOES: Always *add* new potatoes to boiling water. Old potatoes should be started in cold water and brought to a boil.

BISTRO POTATOES

Served with a steak or roast, green beans, and a hearty red wine,
this mashed-potato dish will bring the house down.

INGREDIENTS:
2 pounds Idaho or all-purpose potatoes, peeled
  and quartered
½ cup (1 stick) unsalted butter or margarine
2 medium onions, cut in half lengthwise, then cut
  in thin crescents
Ground nutmeg or pumpkin-pie spice to taste
Freshly ground black pepper to taste

EQUIPMENT:
6-quart stockpot
10-inch sauté pan
3-quart casserole

In just enough water to cover, boil potatoes in stockpot until tender. Drain, let stand 5 minutes, then mash with a fork, leaving them lumpy. Preheat broiler. Melt ⅓ of the butter in sauté pan over medium-high heat, add onions, and sauté until soft, about 10 minutes. Add another ⅓ of the butter; melt, then add mashed potatoes, a generous seasoning of nutmeg and ground pepper, and cook 3 more minutes, stirring frequently.

Put potato mixture in casserole, dot top with pats of remaining butter, and brown lightly under broiler. **Serves 6.**

TIP: If you have an ovenproof sauté pan, you can transfer the potatoes from the stovetop to the broiler in the sauté pan.

If you ever find yourself tempted to MASH POTATOES in your food processor—*don't do it!* They will turn into a starchy glue in seconds.

BOLOGNESE SAUCE

INGREDIENTS:
1 pound lean ground beef
1 tablespoon olive oil
1 green bell pepper, seeded, cored, and chopped
4 ounces mushrooms, trimmed and sliced
1 medium onion, chopped
2 garlic cloves, minced
1 (48-ounce) can whole plum tomatoes, undrained
3 tablespoons tomato paste
¼ cup dry red wine or Marsala
1 tablespoon dried oregano
1 tablespoon dried marjoram
1 tablespoon dried sweet basil
Salt and freshly ground black pepper to taste

EQUIPMENT:
10-inch skillet
3-quart saucepan

In skillet, brown beef over medium heat, breaking up pieces with a spoon. Remove meat to saucepan. Discard fat and wipe skillet with a paper towel. In skillet over medium heat, add oil, green pepper, mushrooms, onion, and garlic and sauté until soft. Add sautéed vegetables to beef in the saucepan, stir in tomatoes, tomato paste, wine, and herbs and bring to a boil. Reduce heat and simmer for at least 1 hour but preferably 2. Add salt and pepper to taste. If you need more liquid, add up to another ¼ cup red wine or water. Serve over pasta of your choice. **Yield: 8 cups.**

QUICK MARINARA

This quick-cooking meatless tomato sauce can be made with either fresh or canned tomatoes. It freezes well, too.

INGREDIENTS:
¾ cup coarsely chopped onion
2 garlic cloves, minced
⅓ cup olive oil
3 pounds ripe Italian plum tomatoes, seeded and chopped or 1 (48-ounce) can plum tomatoes, chopped and drained, reserving 1 cup of juice
½ cup chopped fresh Italian flat-leaf parsley
8 leaves fresh basil, minced, or ½ teaspoon dried sweet basil
1 teaspoon dried oregano
Salt and freshly ground black pepper to taste

EQUIPMENT:
3-quart saucepan

In saucepan over medium heat, sauté onion and garlic in olive oil until onion is wilted. Do not brown. Add tomatoes and remaining ingredients. Bring to a boil, then lower heat to medium and simmer, uncovered, stirring occasionally, 25 to 30 minutes. **Yield: about 8 cups.** ▼ ● ■

THICK AND HEARTY TOMATO SAUCE

Use this all-purpose sauce on pizza or spaghetti.

3 tablespoons olive oil
1½ cups chopped onion
3 garlic cloves, minced
1 (28-ounce) can Italian plum tomatoes, undrained and roughly cut in large chunks
2 (6-ounce) cans tomato paste
2 or more cups water
Salt and freshly ground black pepper to taste
½ teaspoon dried sweet basil
½ teaspoon dried oregano

3-quart saucepan

Heat oil in saucepan over medium heat; add onion and garlic and sauté until golden. Add remaining ingredients and simmer uncovered over low heat about 2 hours, stirring occasionally. Add more water if necessary, but remember—this sauce should be *thick*. **Yield: about 6 cups.** ▼ ● ■

VARIATION: Substitute 1 cup of red wine for 1 cup of the water.

PESTO

Pesto is traditionally used as a sauce for pasta. It's also a delicious addition to soups and many egg dishes.

INGREDIENTS:
2 cups fresh basil leaves
6 large spinach leaves
6 sprigs fresh Italian flat-leaf parsley
3 sprigs fresh marjoram or oregano
½ cup pine nuts or walnuts
⅓ cup grated Parmesan cheese
⅓ cup grated Romano or pecorino cheese
3 tablespoons olive oil
2 tablespoons butter, softened
Salt and freshly ground black pepper to taste

EQUIPMENT:
Food processor or blender

In food processor, process all ingredients at once until no large pieces remain. Don't over-process. Serve at room temperature over hot pasta of your choice. It can also be used on pasta salad served at room temperature. **Yield: about 1 cup.** ▼

TIPS: Pesto can easily be made in advance. It will keep 2 to 3 days, covered in the refrigerator, or can be frozen for 2 to 3 months.

Toasted nuts give the sauce a more robust flavor. Toast on a baking sheet until lightly golden—about 5 minutes in a 350° oven, tossing occasionally.

RED PEPPER SAUCE

This sauce is velvety smooth and wonderful over ravioli or angel-hair pasta. It's also a nice addition to lasagna, pizza, and many vegetable dishes that require tomato sauce. Freeze it in small quantities so that it's always on hand. Use it sparingly, though, because it has a more intense flavor than a tomato sauce.

INGREDIENTS:
3 tablespoons olive oil
1 garlic clove, minced
6 red bell peppers, roasted (see p. 15)
2 teaspoons balsamic vinegar
Salt and freshly ground black pepper to taste

EQUIPMENT:
8-inch sauté pan
Food processor or blender

TIP: Roasted peppers covered with a little olive oil should keep for at least a week in your refrigerator.

In sauté pan, heat 1 tablespoon of the oil over medium-high heat. Add garlic and cook 1 to 2 minutes. Do not brown. Place roasted peppers in food processor with sautéed garlic, remaining olive oil, and vinegar; process until finely blended. Serve at room temperature over pasta or reheat briefly. **Yield: about 3 cups.** ▼ ● ■

VARIATION: Crushed tomatoes can be substituted for some of the peppers. Use 3 to 4 peppers and ½ cup crushed tomatoes.

BASIC BECHAMEL SAUCE

This classic white sauce is the basis for many different dishes and can be varied in many ways. Bechamel Sauce is an essential ingredient in lasagna, and delicious over piquant ravioli.

INGREDIENTS:
¼ cup (½ stick) unsalted butter
3 tablespoons flour
1¾ cups milk
Salt and freshly ground white pepper to taste
Pinch of nutmeg (optional)

EQUIPMENT:
1-quart saucepan

In saucepan, melt butter over medium heat just until bubbling. Do not let it brown. Stir in flour one teaspoon at a time until well blended. Slowly add milk, stirring constantly with a wire whisk, until mixture thickens, about 5 minutes. Season to taste with salt and pepper. **Yield: about 2 cups.**

HERB SAUCE
A variation for vegetables, lasagna and pastas.
To Basic Bechamel Sauce, add 1½ teaspoons minced fresh herbs such as dill, tarragon, parsley, thyme, or ½ teaspoon dried herbs.

SAUCE VELOUTE
Serve over poultry, fish, or beef.
Substitute chicken, fish, or beef stock for the milk in the Basic Bechamel Sauce recipe, then proceed as above.

MUSTARD SAUCE
Serve over vegetables, poultry, white fish.
To Basic Bechamel Sauce, add 3 tablespoons prepared Dijon-style mustard and 1 teaspoon Worcestershire sauce.

MORNAY (CHEESE) SAUCE
Serve over vegetables, toast, white fish.
To Basic Bechamel Sauce, add 4 tablespoons grated Parmesan, Cheddar, Gruyere, or other cheese and stir until cheese is thoroughly melted and blended.

124

Red Pepper Sauce

Stuffed Shells

STUFFED SHELLS

INGREDIENTS:
20 jumbo pasta shells
1 pound fresh spinach
2 cups lean ground turkey or chicken
½ cup grated Parmesan or Romano cheese
½ teaspoon finely grated fresh nutmeg
Salt and freshly ground black pepper to taste
1 teaspoon finely minced garlic
2 large eggs, lightly beaten
¼ cup cream
4 cups Marinara Sauce (see p. 123)

EQUIPMENT:
6-quart stockpot
2-quart covered saucepan
Large (4-quart) mixing bowl
9 × 13-inch baking dish

In stockpot, cook shells al dente according to package directions. Drain well. Place spinach with water clinging to leaves in saucepan, cover tightly, and steam about 5 minutes or until spinach is wilted. Drain, let cool, and chop finely.

In bowl, place turkey, chopped spinach, 4 tablespoons cheese, and remaining ingredients except Marinara Sauce; blend well. Fill shells with mixture.

Preheat oven to 400°. Spoon 1½ cups of Marinara Sauce over bottom of baking pan. Arrange shells in pan and cover with remaining sauce. Sprinkle with the rest of the cheese, and bake 25 minutes. **Serves 4.**

PASTA WITH FRESH TOMATOES

This pasta relies on fresh, superior-quality or homegrown tomatoes. It's extremely simple to prepare, and the sauce cooks in less than 5 minutes.

INGREDIENTS:

1½ pounds penne or rotini, or any tube or corkscrew pasta
1 tablespoon olive oil
2 garlic cloves, minced
1 tablespoon grated onion
4 large fresh tomatoes, chopped, with liquid reserved
¼ cup chopped fresh basil leaves, loosely packed
2 to 3 tablespoons light cream
Salt and freshly ground black pepper to taste
Grated Parmesan cheese (optional)

EQUIPMENT:

8-quart stockpot
10-inch covered sauté pan

VARIATION: To spice up the flavor, add 2 tablespoons of vodka when you add the tomatoes and ¼ teaspoon of cayenne pepper. Cook an additional 2 to 3 minutes to cook off some of the alcohol.

Cook pasta in stockpot according to package directions and drain. Heat oil in sauté pan, add garlic and onion, and sauté less than a minute. Add tomatoes and basil and sauté about 2 more minutes. Add reserved tomato liquid; cover and simmer for another minute. Slowly pour in enough cream to lighten tomato mixture. *Note:* This is not a traditional cream sauce; the cream just adds a touch of flavor. Heat for another minute; add salt and pepper to taste. Toss with pasta, sprinkle with Parmesan cheese, and serve. **Serves 6.** ▼ ● ■

Pasta with Fresh Tomatoes

PASTA WITH GARLIC, CAPERS, AND HERBS

INGREDIENTS:

1½ pounds pasta (orrechietti, fusilli, or radiatore)
½ cup olive oil
8 garlic cloves, minced
⅓ cup capers, drained and rinsed, reserve 2 teaspoons liquid
⅔ cup minced fresh basil leaves
2 tablespoons minced fresh thyme or rosemary leaves
1 teaspoon dried red-pepper flakes
¼ cup grated Parmesan cheese
Fresh basil leaves for garnish

EQUIPMENT:

8-quart stockpot
12-inch sauté pan

Cook the pasta al dente in stockpot according to package directions; drain. In sauté pan, heat oil over medium-low heat. Add garlic and cook 2 minutes. Add capers and caper liquid and cook another minute. To the sauté pan, add pasta, herbs, and red-pepper flakes, tossing well, and cook over medium heat for a few minutes. Remove pasta to a serving dish, toss with Parmesan, and garnish with basil leaves. Serve hot or at room temperature. **Serves 6.** ▼ ● ■

TIP: Be sure to use a pasta with plenty of nooks and crannies so that the herbs, garlic, and capers can hide inside.

See photo, p. 114.

Frutta di Mare Pasta

FRUTTA DI MARE PASTA

INGREDIENTS:

2 pounds large mussels
8 cherrystone clams
6 tablespoons extra-virgin olive oil
4 garlic cloves, finely minced
½ cup dry white wine
2 cups canned whole Italian tomatoes, drained
    but reserving ½ cup juice
1 tablespoon tomato paste
Salt and freshly ground black pepper to taste
½ cup finely chopped Italian flat-leaf parsley
1 pound bay or sea scallops
1 pound medium shrimp, shelled and deveined
1½ pounds fettucine or spaghetti

EQUIPMENT:

2 8-quart stockpots, 1 covered

TIPS: See tip on page 43 for making shrimp broth.

    Try to find the imported tomato paste available in a tube. Although initially more expensive than canned, it is easy to recap, store, and reuse.

    Examine mussels, discard any that are cracked or not tightly closed. Scrub mussels thoroughly under running water, pulling out and discarding fiberlike "beards" from between shells. Scrub clams and place in cold water to cover until ready to use.

    Heat oil in stockpot over medium-heat, add garlic, and sauté just 1 minute. Add wine and simmer 1 more minute. Add all remaining ingredients, including ½ cup reserved tomato juice, except shellfish and pasta. Bring to a boil, then reduce heat and simmer 5 minutes.

    Add clams and mussels to sauce, cover tightly and cook 5 minutes. Add scallops and shrimp and cook covered 5 to 10 minutes more, or until clams and mussels open, scallops are opaque, and shrimp are pink. Do not overcook or shellfish will become tough. Serve over fettucine or spaghetti, cooked according to package directions. **Serves 8.**

PASTA VERDURE

You can serve this dish piping hot or at room temperature.

INGREDIENTS:
½ pound angel-hair pasta
2 garlic cloves, minced
3 tablespoons olive oil
4 cups broccoli florets, cut in 1-inch pieces, about
    1 pound
¼ cup water
8 ounces fresh mushrooms, trimmed and
    quartered
½ medium red bell pepper, cored, seeded, and
    diced
½ medium yellow bell pepper, cored, seeded,
    and diced
10 ounces fresh spinach, torn into small pieces
3 small zucchini, sliced into ½-inch rounds
Salt and freshly ground black pepper to taste
Grated Parmesan or Romano cheese

EQUIPMENT:
3-quart saucepan
12-inch covered sauté pan or sautôir

Cook pasta in saucepan according to package directions and drain. In sauté pan, heat oil over medium heat, add garlic, and sauté 1 to 2 minutes. Add broccoli and water, cover, and steam approximately 3 minutes. Most of the water will evaporate. Add mushrooms and peppers and mix well. Add spinach, still wet from washing, and zucchini slices. Season with salt and pepper. Cover and cook 3 to 4 minutes, or until spinach is wilted and zucchini is tender-crisp. *Do not overcook.*

Place pasta in a serving bowl. Combine with vegetable mixture, toss lightly, and serve with cheese on the side. **Serves 4 to 6.** ▼ ● ■

PADELLATO

This pasta is first slightly undercooked in water, drained, then tossed with sauce in a large sauté pan the way many authentic Italian dishes are prepared.

INGREDIENTS:
4 small sweet or hot Italian sausages (or
    "breakfast" type pork link sausage)
5 tablespoons vegetable or olive oil
1 large onion, thickly sliced
1 large green bell pepper, cored, seeded, and
    cut in slices about the size of the pasta
1 tablespoon chopped fresh basil leaves or 1
    teaspoon dried sweet basil
1 (28-ounce) can Italian plum tomatoes, quartered,
    drained, and liquid reserved.
½ pound short pasta such as ziti, penne, or
    rotelle
½ cup grated pecorino, Romano or Parmesan
    cheese

EQUIPMENT:
10-inch sauté pan or 12-inch sautôir
3-quart saucepan

TIPS: *Al dente* literally means "to the tooth"; it should be tender yet show a little white core when bitten in half.

By using half a yellow and half a green pepper you create a colorful dish.

In sauté pan over low heat, cook sausages in 2 tablespoons of the oil, pricking them with a fork so that they lose a little fat. After 10 to 15 minutes, remove sausages, slice into ½-inch-thick pieces, and set aside.

Pour off fat from sauté pan; add remaining oil, and sauté onion over medium-high heat about 4 to 5 minutes or until golden. Add green pepper and continue sautéing until pepper softens slightly. Reduce heat to medium, add basil, tomatoes, ¼ cup tomato liquid, and reserved sausage pieces. Bring to a gentle boil; reduce heat, cover, and cook 10 minutes. Add a little more of the tomato liquid if the mixture becomes dry.

Cook pasta al dente according to package directions. Drain well. Increase heat under sauté pan and add pasta, tossing gently and continuously until pasta is well covered with sauce and cooked a little more, about 2 to 3 minutes. Sprinkle with cheese and serve. **Serves 4.**

No-Boil Lasagna Primavera

NO-BOIL LASAGNA PRIMAVERA

It's a fact—it isn't necessary to boil the pasta before assembling this tasty dish. You don't even need to buy pasta that is specifically labeled "no-boil"—any variety will do. The secret is in adding slightly more liquid to the recipe than is usually called for.

INGREDIENTS:

1 large red onion, thinly sliced
3 tablespoons olive oil
1 small summer squash, sliced into ¼-inch rounds
1 small zucchini, sliced into ¼-inch rounds
1 small green bell pepper, seeded, cored, and thinly sliced
8 stalks asparagus, tough ends removed, chopped into 1-inch lengths
1 small red bell pepper, seeded, cored, and thinly sliced
⅔ cup vegetable broth or dry white wine
3¾ cups Marinara Sauce (see p. 123)
8 ounces lasagna noodles
2 cups Herb Bechamel Sauce (see p. 124), using 1 teaspoon minced fresh thyme and ½ teaspoon minced fresh tarragon
½ cup grated Parmesan cheese
8 ounces mozzarella cheese, shredded

EQUIPMENT:

10-inch sauté pan
2-quart saucepan
9 × 13-inch baking dish

Preheat oven to 350°. In sauté pan over medium heat, cook onion in oil until just wilted. Add summer squash, zucchini, green pepper, and asparagus and cook 5 to 8 minutes, stirring constantly. Add red pepper, cook 5 more minutes, and set aside.

In saucepan, add broth to Marinara Sauce and blend thoroughly. Simmer over medium heat until heated through. Cover bottom of baking dish with 1⅓ cups of the Marinara Sauce. Lay half of the *uncooked* lasagna noodles over the sauce and cover with the vegetables. Pour 1 cup of the Herb Bechamel Sauce over vegetables and sprinkle with half the Parmesan cheese. Top with 1 cup Marinara Sauce and add another layer of lasagna. Spread the rest of the Bechamel Sauce over the lasagna, sprinkle with remaining Parmesan, and cover with the rest of the Marinara Sauce. Sprinkle with mozzarella. Cover pan with aluminum foil and bake 30 minutes. Remove foil cover and bake 15 more minutes or until bubbly and golden brown. **Serves 6.** ▼

Spicy Szechuan Noodles

SPICY SZECHUAN NOODLES

INGREDIENTS:
1 pound Chinese egg noodles
3 tablespoons dark sesame oil
3 tablespoons soy sauce
3 tablespoons rice-wine vinegar
4 teaspoons sugar
1 teaspoon hot chili oil
2 teaspoons grated fresh ginger
¼ cup sliced scallions, white and tender greens
½ cup grated carrots
½ cup sliced enoki mushrooms (optional)
2 stalks celery, trimmed and julienned
Salt and freshly ground black pepper to taste

EQUIPMENT:
6-quart stockpot
Large serving bowl
Small (1-quart) mixing bowl

In stockpot, cook noodles according to package directions and drain. Place noodles in large serving bowl and toss with sesame oil. In small bowl combine soy sauce, vinegar, sugar, chili oil, and ginger. Pour over noodles, mix, and allow to cool to room temperature. Add vegetables, salt, and pepper and serve. **Serves 6.** ▼ ● ■

TIP: You can prepare the noodles and combine with dressing up to a day ahead of time and store in refrigerator. Three hours before serving, remove from refrigerator; add vegetables and toss.

130

HALLOWEEN TREATS FOR TRICKSTERS

Tutti-Frutti Punch
Halloween Nachos
Presto Pizza
Carrot Cupcakes

Carrot Cupcakes and *Tutti-Frutti Punch*

To minimize wear and tear on the cook (you), most of the items on the menu provided above can be partially or entirely prepared a day in advance.

We suggest using *Thick and Hearty Tomato Sauce* (see p. 123) on the *Presto Pizza*. If you make the sauce ahead of time and freeze it, all you'll have to do is allow it to thaw. The pizza dough (see p. 135) can be prepared the day before the party. After kneading, refrigerate in tightly covered container until you're ready to make the pizzas. Then knead again and proceed with the recipe. Spoon on the tomato sauce, and let your kids choose the toppings they like best.

Also on the day before the party, make the *Carrot Cupcakes* following the recipe for *Carrot Cake* (see p. 150) but using muffin tins with paper liners instead of a cake pan. (It should make about 20 cupcakes.) Fill each cup halfway and bake 25 to 30 minutes, or until a toothpick inserted in the center comes out clean. Make frosting (see p. 150) and after the cupcakes have cooled, frost them. Decorate with orange sprinkles or candy corn. Your kids will have fun helping with this!

For *Halloween Nachos*, you'll need a large bag of tortilla chips, 12 to 14 ounces Cheddar or Monterey Jack cheese, and about 1 cup salsa. The day before the party, shred the cheese and refrigerate in a plastic bag. Right before you plan to serve them, prepare the nachos. Preheat oven to Broil. Spread the tortilla chips on a large baking sheet and spoon about ½ cup salsa over them. Sprinkle liberally with grated cheese and place under the broiler just until cheese melts, about 5 minutes. Serve with remaining salsa.

The day of the party, make *Tutti-Frutti Punch*. Combine 1 quart orange juice with 1 pint cranberry juice and 1 pint ginger ale. Fizzy, festive, and fun!

BREADS, EGGS, SANDWICHES

This potpourri of breads and muffins, delicious egg dishes, and extraordinary tea sandwiches will round out your cooking basics for every meal. Serve them for breakfast, brunch, and lunch, of course. Most are delicious with dinner, too.

BANANA-FIG BREAD

INGREDIENTS:
1¾ cups all-purpose flour
1 tablespoon baking powder
½ cup sugar
⅓ cup butter or margarine
2 eggs
3 medium bananas, about 1 cup, mashed
1 teaspoon grated orange rind
¼ cup finely chopped dried figs

EQUIPMENT:
Large (4-quart) mixing bowl
Small (1½-quart) mixing bowl
1½-quart loaf pan

Preheat oven to 350°. Into large bowl sift together flour and baking powder. In small bowl beat sugar and butter together until creamy. Add eggs and beat until well blended. Add egg mixture to dry ingredients. Stir just until smooth. Add bananas, orange rind, and figs; stir again. Pour into greased loaf pan. Bake 45 minutes or until firmly set when lightly touched on center top. Cool on rack. Remove from pan after 10 minutes. **Yield: 1 loaf.**

TIP: Toss figs with sugar or some flour to make them easier to chop.

JALAPEÑO CHEESE BISCUITS

INGREDIENTS:
1½ cups sifted all-purpose flour
4 teaspoons baking powder
½ teaspoon salt
½ cup uncooked corn grits or cornmeal
¼ cup butter or margarine, softened
1 jalapeño pepper, seeded and finely diced
1 cup grated Cheddar cheese
⅓ cup or more milk

EQUIPMENT:
Medium (2½-quart) mixing bowl
Baking sheet

Preheat oven to 425°. Mix flour, baking powder, salt, and grits in bowl. Cut in butter with a fork or pastry blender until crumbly. Stir in jalapeño pepper and cheese, slowly add ⅓ cup milk, and stir lightly. Add more milk, 1 tablespoon at a time, if needed to make dough hold together.

Put dough on lightly floured board or canvas. Knead gently a few times. Roll dough into a 9 × 8-inch rectangle. With sharp knife, cut into eight 1-inch-wide strips. Cut each strip crosswise into three 3-inch pieces. Place about one inch apart on ungreased baking sheet. Bake for 12 minutes or until lightly browned. **Yield: 24 biscuits.**

BAKING POWDER can lose its zip if stored for long periods. Invest in a new can (and date the top of the new one) if you haven't baked in a while.

Banana-Fig Bread

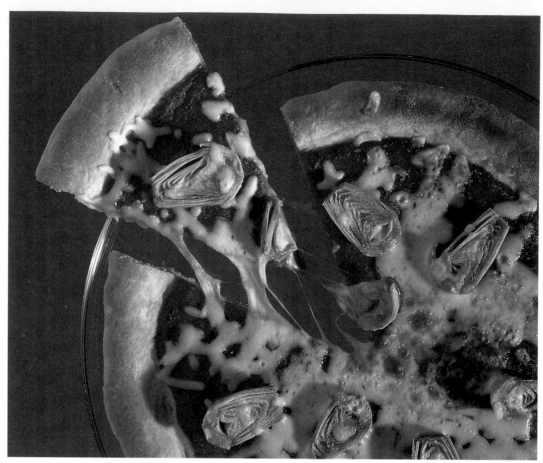

Artichoke
Presto
Pizza

Apple-Bran Muffins

PRESTO PIZZA

A no-yeast pizza dough that's ready to bake in less than 10 minutes. For appetizers, instead of making one large pizza, cut the dough into small circles with a cookie cutter.

INGREDIENTS:
2¼ cups all-purpose flour
1½ tablespoons baking powder
1 teaspoon salt
8 tablespoons olive oil
⅔ cup water

EQUIPMENT:
Large (4-quart) mixing bowl
12- to 14-inch pizza pan or baking sheet

Preheat oven to 450°. Sift dry ingredients into bowl. Add water and 6 tablespoons oil; mix with your hands until ingredients form a soft dough. Put dough on lightly floured surface and knead gently about 30 seconds. Press or roll dough into a flat circle about ⅛-inch thick. Turn up edges to make a rim, place on ungreased pizza pan, and brush with remaining 2 tablespoons olive oil. Let stand 5 minutes. Add toppings of choice and bake as indicated below. **Yield: 1 pizza.**

SUGGESTED TOPPINGS

Pizza Classico: Grated fresh mozzarella cheese, Thick and Hearty Tomato Sauce (see p. 123), slivered green bell peppers, freshly grated Parmesan or Romano cheese, dried oregano or marjoram, and olive oil. Cover with tomato sauce, sprinkle with mozzarella, add pepper slivers, sprinkle with Parmesan or Romano cheese and herbs. Drizzle lightly with olive oil; bake 15 minutes. ▼

Artichoke Pizza: Slices of fresh mozzarella cheese, Red Pepper Sauce (see p. 124), sautéed or steamed artichoke hearts, sliced, and olive oil. Cover pizza with sauce, arrange slices of mozzarella and artichoke hearts on top, drizzle with olive oil; bake 15 minutes. ▼

Pizza alla Pesto: Steamed spinach, grated Parmesan or Romano cheese, Pesto Sauce (see p. 123). After brushing pizza with olive oil, bake for 10 minutes or until golden. Remove from oven, spread with half of the pesto, cover with spinach, sprinkle with grated cheese, and "dot" with remaining pesto. Return to oven and bake 2 to 3 more minutes. ▼

Pizza Fresco: Chopped fresh tomatoes, chopped fresh basil leaves, salt and pepper to taste, and fresh mozzarella slices. Cover pizza with chopped tomatoes, sprinkle with basil, season with salt and pepper, and cover with mozzarella slices; bake 15 minutes. ▼

APPLE-BRAN MUFFINS

INGREDIENTS:
1½ cups oat bran
¾ cup rice bran
1½ teaspoons ground cinnamon
1 tablespoon baking powder
1 cup raisins
1 large apple, peeled, cored, and diced
¼ cup sugar
½ cup skim milk
¾ cup apple juice or cider
2 egg whites
2 tablespoons vegetable oil

EQUIPMENT:
Large (4-quart) mixing bowl
Small (1½-quart) mixing bowl
Muffin pan for 12 muffins

Preheat oven to 425°. Mix together the dry ingredients and fruit in large bowl. Beat together remaining ingredients in small bowl; add to dry ingredients and fruit and stir until moistened. Pour batter into muffin pan lined with paper muffin cups and bake 17 minutes. **Yield: 12 muffins.** ● ■

FLOUR TORTILLAS

Homemade tortillas are lower in fat than the store-bought variety. Serve them instead of bread with Hot and Spicy Black Bean Soup (see p. 38).

INGREDIENTS:
3 cups unbleached all-purpose flour
⅓ cup vegetable oil (corn, safflower, or olive)
1 teaspoon salt
1 cup warm water

EQUIPMENT:
Large (4-quart) mixing bowl
10-inch heavy cast-iron pan or griddle

TIP: You can prepare the dough a day ahead of time to the point where it is finished resting. Wrap it in plastic and store it in the refrigerator, not more than 24 hours. Or you can roll out the tortillas and layer wax paper between them, cover with plastic wrap, and store in the refrigerator overnight.

In mixing bowl, combine flour and oil by hand or fork until evenly mixed and crumbly. Combine salt and water, add it to the flour, and mix by hand until a ball can be formed with the dough. Place dough on a lightly floured board and knead until smooth and elastic (about 5 minutes). Return dough to mixing bowl and cover with a slightly damp towel. Turn oven on to its lowest setting for 2 minutes, then turn off the heat. Put covered bowl in oven and let it rest 30 minutes to 2 hours.

Divide dough into 12 equal pieces and roll each between your palms to form balls roughly the size of golf balls. Flatten each ball between your palms and lay it on a lightly floured work surface. With a rolling pin, roll each ball out to a thin 8-inch round. Layer uncooked tortillas on a plate with a piece of wax paper between each.

Over high heat, heat pan until hot; lower heat to medium-high and place tortilla in pan. Cook each side for 30 seconds. The cooked tortilla should have small brown spots and be flexible, not crisp. Stack tortillas as they are cooked and use them immediately, or keep them warm in the oven. **Yield: 12 tortillas.**

CORN BREAD

INGREDIENTS:
2 cups cornmeal
1 tablespoon baking powder
¼ teaspoon salt
1 egg, lightly beaten
1 cup milk
2 tablespoons honey
¼ cup vegetable oil

EQUIPMENT:
Medium (2½-quart) mixing bowl
Small (1-quart) mixing bowl
8-inch square baking pan

Preheat oven to 400°. Mix together thoroughly cornmeal, baking powder, and salt in medium bowl. Mix egg, milk, honey, and oil in small bowl. Add to cornmeal mixture. Stir only until dry ingredients are moistened; batter will be lumpy. Pour into greased baking pan and bake 20 minutes or until lightly browned. **Serves 4 to 6.**

TIP: Substitute 2 egg whites for the egg and use skim milk to significantly reduce cholesterol and fat.

ENGLISH SCONES

INGREDIENTS:
2 cups unbleached all-purpose flour
6 tablespoons sugar
1 tablespoon baking powder
½ teaspoon salt
6 tablespoons butter, cold
1 egg
1 cup cream or whole milk
½ cup currants, raisins, or chocolate chips
   (optional)

EQUIPMENT:
Large (4-quart) mixing bowl
Small (1½-quart) mixing bowl
Baking sheet

TIP: Do not try to substitute margarine for butter when making scones as it will adversely affect the consistency of the dough.

See photo, p. 161.

Preheat oven to 400°. Mix together dry ingredients in large bowl. Cut butter into small pieces and scatter them into dry mixture. Using the tips of your fingers, break butter into pieces the size of a small pea. In small bowl, beat egg, add cream. Reserve 2 tablespoons of egg mixture to use later for brushing on top of the scones. Add currants, raisins, or chocolate chips to egg mixture.

Pour wet ingredients into flour mixture and stir until the liquid is just incorporated. The dough should be soft and slightly sticky. If the dough sticks to your fingers, correct the texture by adding a tablespoon of flour at a time. If it's stiff and doesn't hold together, add cream a tablespoon at a time.

Divide dough in half and shape into two balls. Place each ball on either end of a lightly greased baking sheet and press down to form into circles about 6 inches across and 1 inch thick. Cut each circle of dough into six wedges and pull wedges slightly away from one another. Lightly brush with reserved egg mixture. Bake about 12 minutes or until the scones are lightly browned. **Yield: 12 scones.**

CHIVE SPOON BREAD

Serve with grilled or roasted chicken or meats.

INGREDIENTS:
1 cup milk
3 tablespoons butter or margarine, melted
⅓ cup white cornmeal
1 teaspoon baking powder
1 teaspoon sugar
¼ teaspoon salt
2 eggs, well beaten
2 tablespoons chopped chives

EQUIPMENT:
Medium (2½-quart) mixing bowl
1½-quart casserole

Preheat oven to 350°. Combine milk and butter in a bowl. Stir in cornmeal, baking powder, sugar, and salt. Stir in eggs and chives until well blended. Pour batter into greased casserole dish and bake 30 to 40 minutes. Bread is done when a wooden pick inserted near center comes out clean. Let stand about 5 minutes, then serve at once. **Serves 4 to 6.**

Chive Spoon Bread

PUMPKIN BREAD

INGREDIENTS:
¼ cup vegetable oil
¼ cup melted butter or margarine
¾ cup sugar
1 egg
1 cup pumpkin puree (not pumpkin-pie filling),
  canned
1 cup grated, unpeeled apple
2 cups all-purpose flour
1 teaspoon baking soda
½ teaspoon baking powder
¼ teaspoon salt
½ teaspoon cinnamon
¼ cup sesame seeds or chopped nuts (optional)
½ cup raisins (optional)
Topping:
2 tablespoons butter
2 tablespoons sugar
2 tablespoons flour
½ teaspoon cinnamon

EQUIPMENT:
Large (4-quart) mixing bowl
2 small (1-quart) mixing bowls
1½-quart loaf pan

Preheat oven to 350°. In large bowl, mix together oil, butter, sugar, egg, pumpkin puree, and apple. In smaller bowl, mix together flour, baking soda, baking powder, salt, and cinnamon. Add flour mixture to pumpkin and stir until well moistened. Fold in sesame seeds, nuts, or raisins, and spoon into greased loaf pan.

In a small bowl and using your fingers, blend topping ingredients together until they form a coarse meal. Sprinkle on top of loaf. Bake 40 minutes or until toothpick inserted in center comes out clean. Remove from pan and cool on rack. **Yield: 1 loaf.**

Italian Bread with Olive Oil and Herbs

ITALIAN BREAD WITH OLIVE OIL AND HERBS

Healthier than buttered garlic bread and just as delicious.

INGREDIENTS:
½ cup extra-virgin olive oil
1 teaspoon mixed dried herbs, oregano,
  marjoram, and thyme
Pinch of salt
1 loaf Italian bread
Grated Parmesan cheese (optional)

EQUIPMENT:
Small bowl or 2-cup measuring cup
Baking sheet

Preheat oven to Broil. Whisk olive oil, herbs, and salt in bowl until thoroughly blended. Slice bread in half lengthwise, and drizzle olive-oil mixture over both cut surfaces. (If loaf is exceptionally large, you may need to increase quantities of oil and herbs.) Place bread on baking sheet; broil, cut-sides up, for 1 to 2 minutes or until surface of bread is lightly browned. Serve warm. Sprinkle with cheese if desired. **Serves 6.**

TEA SANDWICHES

DAIKON AND CREAM CHEESE

INGREDIENTS:
3 ounces cream cheese or Neufchâtel
2 teaspoons chopped fresh dill
½ daikon radish, thinly sliced
6 thin slices rye bread, crusts trimmed

Blend cream cheese with fresh dill. Spread cheese mixture evenly on 3 slices of the bread. Add daikon slices cut to fit bread and top with remaining bread. Cut each sandwich into quarters. **Yield: 12 sandwiches.**

SMOKED TROUT AND APPLE

INGREDIENTS:
2 teaspoons unsalted butter
3 ounces thinly sliced smoked trout
2 Granny Smith apples, peeled, cored, and thinly sliced
6 thin slices black bread, crusts trimmed

Spread butter lightly on bread. Top 3 slices with smoked trout and apple slices cut to fit bread. Top with remaining bread and cut sandwiches into quarters. **Yield: 12 sandwiches.**

Assorted Tea Sandwiches

STILTON AND PEAR

INGREDIENTS:
3 ounces Stilton cheese
2 firm, ripe pears (preferably comice or nelice), peeled, cored, and thinly sliced
6 thin slices brown bread, crusts trimmed

Spread Stilton cheese evenly on 3 slices of the bread. Top with pear slices, cut to fit bread. Top with remaining bread and cut each sandwich into quarters. **Yield: 12 sandwiches.**

BAKED EGGS ITALIANO

We recommend serving one egg per person with fresh fruit, toast, or English muffin.

INGREDIENTS:
1 teaspoon olive oil
6 thin slices of cooked ham, cut to fit dish
2 tablespoons Pesto (see p. 123)
6 eggs
4 ounces mozzarella cheese, grated

EQUIPMENT:
6 ramekins

See photo, p. 161.

Preheat oven to 400°. Grease each ramekin with olive oil. Inside, place a ham slice spread with 1 to 2 teaspoons Pesto. Crack one egg on top (two if you wish), sprinkle with grated mozzarella and bake for 6 minutes or until eggs are firm. **Serves 6.**

TIP: You can substitute prosciutto or peppered ham for the cooked ham. Prepared pesto sauce can also be used if homemade is not available.

BROCCOLI FRITTATA

A versatile dish is the frittata, an omelet that is made on top of the stove then popped into the oven to finish. Be sure you have the proper pan—one that can go straight from the stove top to oven. Broccoli is a favorite frittata ingredient. Use it, but do try improvising as well. Frittatas are a terrific way to use a variety of leftovers. Like quiche, frittatas can be served hot or at room temperature. They are just as good coming out of a picnic basket as they are straight from the oven.

INGREDIENTS:

1 pound broccoli, peeled, trimmed and cut into
   ½-inch slices
¼ cup olive or vegetable oil
½ pound fresh mushrooms, trimmed and sliced
2 garlic cloves, minced
Pinch of salt
¾ teaspoon freshly ground black pepper
8 eggs
½ cup grated Parmesan cheese
1 red bell pepper, seeded, cored, and cut in
   strips

EQUIPMENT:

10-inch covered ovenproof skillet
Medium (2½-quart) mixing bowl

Preheat oven to 350°. Steam broccoli, covered, in skillet for 2 to 3 minutes in 2 tablespoons water or in the microwave oven for about 1½ minutes: Drain well. Heat oil in skillet over medium heat, add broccoli, mushrooms, and garlic. Stir, cover, and cook 3 minutes. In bowl combine salt, pepper, and eggs, beat lightly, and pour over broccoli. Sprinkle with Parmesan cheese, arrange pepper strips in a spokelike fashion on top, and bake, uncovered, 15 to 20 minutes or until just set but not dry. **Serves 6.** ▼

VARIATION: Before baking, add to the eggs ½ cup grated Monterey Jack or Muenster cheese instead of Parmesan.

ARTICHOKE FRITTATA

INGREDIENTS:

2 tablespoons olive oil
1 (10-ounce) package frozen artichoke hearts,
   thawed and chopped
⅓ pound fresh mushrooms, trimmed and sliced
1 onion, thinly sliced
1 garlic clove, minced
½ teaspoon dried sweet basil
Salt and freshly ground black pepper to taste
⅓ cup chopped fresh parsley
½ cup grated Parmesan cheese
6 eggs, beaten

EQUIPMENT:

8-inch ovenproof skillet
Medium (2½-quart) mixing bowl

Preheat oven to 350°. In skillet over medium-low heat, heat oil a minute or two, then add artichokes, mushrooms, onions, garlic, basil, salt, and pepper. Stir to mix, cover, and cook 5 minutes. In bowl combine eggs, parsley, and most of the cheese, pour over vegetables. Sprinkle rest of cheese on top and bake 15 to 20 minutes or until just set but not dry. **Serves 4.** ▼

TIP: You can also use canned, water-packed artichokes (8½ ounces). Drain well, chop, and sprinkle with a little lemon juice. Add to skillet after the egg mixture and stir gently.

HAM-AND-CHEESE-ON-RYE STRATA

Serve with grapefruit or an endive-and-watercress salad.

INGREDIENTS:
½ pound cooked ham, cut into ½-inch cubes
8 slices seeded or unseeded rye bread, cut into 1-inch cubes
¾ pound Montery Jack cheese, coarsely grated
4 eggs, lightly beaten
1½ cups milk
Salt and freshly ground black pepper to taste
1 teaspoon Dijon-style mustard
Pinch of cayenne or a few drops of Tabasco sauce
½ teaspoon Worcestershire sauce
⅓ cup finely chopped scallions, white and tender greens

EQUIPMENT:
9 × 13-inch baking pan
Medium (2½-quart) mixing bowl

Combine ham and bread cubes and spread in greased baking pan. Sprinkle with half the grated cheese. Mix together remaining ingredients in bowl and pour over ham, bread, and cheese. Top with remaining cheese and refrigerate at least 2 hours, preferably overnight.

Approximately 30 minutes before baking, remove strata from refrigerator and preheat oven to 325°. Bake for 45 minutes, or until surface is golden-brown. Let "rest" 10 minutes before serving. **Serves 4 to 6.**

SUNDAY SCRAMBLED EGGS

You can have creamy scrambled eggs without undercooking the eggs. The trick is to cook them slowly. Because they are so rich, you don't need two eggs per person.

INGREDIENTS:
1 tablespoon butter or margarine
1 bunch scallions, white and tender greens, sliced
9 eggs
1 tablespoon water
5 to 6 ounces cream cheese or Neufchâtel, cut in ½-inch cubes
Salt and freshly ground black pepper to taste

EQUIPMENT:
2-quart saucepan
Medium (2½-quart) mixing bowl

TIP: A tablespoon of chopped chives can be substituted for the scallions if you prefer. Add directly to egg mixture.

Melt butter in saucepan over low heat. Sauté scallions about 2 minutes until limp. Whisk together eggs and water in bowl and pour into saucepan, stirring frequently over low heat for about 10 minutes. Use a saucepan, not a skillet, so that the egg mixture will be deep and cook slowly. The lower the flame and the more frequently you stir, the smoother the eggs will be.

When eggs have reached desired consistency, turn off heat and quickly stir in cream cheese. Cream cheese should melt slightly but not be completely blended into eggs. Salt and pepper to taste. **Serves 6.**

EGGS: If you're concerned about the possibility of salmonella contamination in recipes containing eggs, the U.S. Department of Agriculture states that heating to a temperature of 160° or above will destroy the organisms. You can use a meat thermometer to determine the exact temperature.

QUICK AND EASY QUICHE

Quiche can be served as a main dish or in smaller slices as an hors d'oeuvre. For a crowd, make several different quiches so that guests can pick and choose.

INGREDIENTS:
10-inch unbaked piecrust, fresh or frozen
Basic custard:
3 eggs
1½ cups light cream
Salt and freshly ground black pepper to taste
Pinch of nutmeg

EQUIPMENT:
Medium (2½-quart) mixing bowl

Beat eggs and cream until thoroughly blended; season with salt, pepper, and nutmeg. This custard can be used immediately or frozen for future use. The recipe makes 2 cups, enough for a 10-inch pie.

To assemble quiche, bake piecrust in 375° oven 15 minutes. Cool slightly, then fill with any of the ingredients suggested below. Lower oven temperature to 350°; pour custard over filling and bake 40 to 45 minutes, or until custard is firm and crust is lightly browned. To determine if custard is cooked all the way through, insert a knife blade into center of filling. If blade comes out clean, custard is done. **Serves 6 as main course; 10 to 12 as hors d'oeuvre.**
▼

Ratatouille Quiche

SUGGESTED FILLINGS (2 to 3 cups)

Quiche Lorraine: ½ pound bacon, fried until crisp and then crumbled; 4 large yellow onions, thinly sliced and sautéed in butter until golden; 6 ounces Gruyère cheese, cut into small cubes. Combine all ingredients, place in prepared pie shell, cover with custard, and bake as above.

Ratatouille Quiche: ¼ cup olive oil; 2 medium onions, sliced; 2 garlic cloves, chopped; 1 small eggplant, peeled and cubed; 1 medium green bell pepper, seeded, cored, and cut into thin strips; 2 small zucchini, sliced; 4 fresh plum tomatoes, sliced; 1 teaspoon dried oregano. In large skillet over medium heat, sauté onions and garlic in olive oil, stirring occasionally until onions begin to soften. Add eggplant and green pepper; continue cooking, still stirring, 2 to 3 minutes. Add remaining ingredients, cover and cook 5 more minutes. Remove from heat, uncover, and let cool to room temperature. Place mixture in prepared crust, cover with custard, and bake as above. ▼

Mushroom Quiche: 1 pound fresh mushrooms, trimmed and sliced; 4 tablespoons unsalted butter. Sauté mushrooms in butter over medium heat until just tender, about 5 minutes. Place mushrooms in prepared crust, cover with custard, and bake as above. ▼

FALL AND WINTER HOLIDAY FEAST

Curried Ginger-Pumpkin Soup
Winter Holiday Salad
Roast Turkey with Herb or Oyster Stuffing
Fresh Cranberry-Orange Relish
Cornbread
Garlic and Herb Mashed Potatoes
Broccoli with Lemon-Chive Sauce
Pear-Cranberry Crumble
Ginger Cookies

Roasted Turkey, (see p. 54), Broccoli with Lemon-Chive Sauce, (see p. 100), and Herb Stuffing (see p. 52.)

Whether the frost is on the pumpkin or the snow is on the ground, as the year draws to a close, it's a time-honored American custom to gather together with family and friends in celebration. 'Tis the season to enjoy a truly magnificent meal, and on those festive occasions, even the most health-conscious of us tend to throw dietary caution to the winds for just one day.

But believe it or not, a delicious holiday dinner doesn't have to break the calorie bank or raise your cholesterol level to stratospheric heights. Though the menu we've devised incorporates the mouth-watering dishes traditionally associated with fall and winter feasting, they are all prepared with a contemporary regard for good nutrition.

So set the table with your finest linens, china, crystal, and silver, arrange a festive centerpiece, light the candles, and treat yourself and your guests to a luscious holiday meal you can enjoy without a single morsel of guilt.

DESSERTS

Desserts need no introduction—not even a meal before them. Our only advice is that you should not consume a dessert every day—unless it's Banana "Ice Cream" (see p. 154). We have, however, provided a number of lower-in-calorie, lower-in-fat alternatives to overly rich delicacies that can be just as satisfying and a lot more conducive to healthy eating. Enjoy them in moderation.

BROWN SUGAR AND STRAWBERRY

SHORTCAKE

INGREDIENTS:
1½ cups all-purpose flour
1 tablespoon baking powder
¼ teaspoon baking soda
¼ cup sugar
Dash of salt
⅓ cup solid shortening, unsalted butter, or
   margarine
1 egg
¾ cup milk
Topping:
4 cups (1 quart) fresh strawberries
1 cup plain yogurt or sour cream
¼ cup firmly packed light brown sugar

EQUIPMENT:
2 small (1-quart) mixing bowls
Medium (2½-quart) mixing bowl
Cookie sheet

For topping, remove stems from strawberries and cut in half lengthwise. Place in small bowl and set aside. Do this step first if you plan to serve shortcake as soon as it is baked because berries need about an hour to develop some juice.

Preheat oven to 400°. Sift together flour, baking powder, baking soda, sugar, and salt in medium bowl. Cut in shortening with a fork or pastry blender. Mix together egg and milk in small bowl; gradually add to flour mixture. You may not need all the liquid; dough should hold together in a ball.

To make individual shortcakes, pat dough into a rectangle about ¾-inch thick. Cut into 6 rounds with knife or cookie cutter, using all the dough. Place rounds on cookie sheet and bake 10 to 12 minutes or until golden.

Lightly mix together the yogurt and brown sugar. Cut each cooled shortcake in half. Place strawberries and some of the yogurt on bottom half. Replace top half of shortcake and top with remaining strawberries and yogurt. **Serves 6.**

> EGG WHITES can be kept frozen for several weeks; they will also keep for about a week in the refrigerator. Egg yolks cannot be frozen but will keep for 3 to 4 days in the refrigerator if covered with a little water.

Brown Sugar and Strawberry Shortcake

GINGER COOKIES

INGREDIENTS:

¼ cup butter or margarine
½ cup firmly packed light or dark brown sugar
½ cup dark molasses
3½ cups all-purpose flour
1 teaspoon baking soda
1 teaspoon ground cinnamon
2 teaspoons ground ginger
¼ teaspoon nutmeg
Pinch of salt
⅓ cup water

EQUIPMENT:

2 medium (2½-quart) mixing bowls
Rolling pin
Cookie sheet

In bowl, cream together butter and brown sugar; beat in molasses. Combine flour, baking soda, spices and salt in other bowl. Add to sugar mixture one-third at a time, alternating with water. Stir until blended. Form dough into ball; cover with plastic wrap and refrigerate 3 hours.

Preheat oven to 350°. Roll out dough to ¼-inch thickness on lightly floured surface. Cut out cookies in desired shapes. Bake for 12 to 15 minutes on greased or nonstick cookie sheet. Cool on rack. **Yield: about 2 dozen cookies.**

FREEZER CURRIED COOKIES

Because the dough in this recipe is frozen before baking, it can be prepared ahead of time and the cookies baked fresh when you want them. Serve with Poached Pears (see p. 160).

INGREDIENTS:

1½ cups walnuts
2 cups firmly packed brown sugar
3 cups all-purpose flour
½ teaspoon baking soda
1 teaspoon baking powder
½ teaspoon salt (optional)
2 teaspoons curry powder
1 cup (2 sticks) butter or margarine, cold and cut in tablespoon-sized pieces
2 eggs, beaten
2 teaspoons vanilla extract

EQUIPMENT:

Food processor
Cookie sheet

Process walnuts and brown sugar in food processor 45 seconds until crumbly. Add flour, baking soda, baking powder, salt, and curry powder and process 30 seconds or until thoroughly mixed. Add cold butter pieces and process until crumbly. Add eggs and vanilla and pulse until mixed. Place mixture on lightly floured surface and divide into 4 logs. Wrap each in plastic wrap and freeze. To bake, remove logs from freezer, thaw and cut into ¼-inch-thick slices.

Preheat oven to 300°. Line the cookie sheet with baker's (parchment) paper; arrange four rows of six cookies each and bake 16 to 18 minutes. Remove from oven and slip off paper with cookies on it; allow to cool before removing cookies. **Yield: 96 cookies.**

TIP: Ginger Cookies, Freezer Curried Cookies (above), and Perfect Pumpkin Cake (see p. 152) form a delightful trio of desserts for a fall or winter buffet.

Tip: To make slices without pinching the log, loop waxed dental floss around log and pull ends to make uniform slices.

Ginger Cookies

Pear-Cranberry Crumble

PEAR-CRANBERRY CRUMBLE

INGREDIENTS:

4 large firm, ripe pears, peeled, cored, and sliced
12 ounces cranberries, rinsed and picked over to remove stems
⅓ cup sugar
½ teaspoon cinnamon
¾ cup rolled oats (not instant)
⅔ cup firmly packed brown sugar
½ cup (1 stick) butter or margarine, cut into ½-inch pieces
½ cup all-purpose flour

EQUIPMENT:

10-inch pie plate or quiche dish
Medium (2½-quart) mixing bowl

Preheat oven to 375°. Toss pears, cranberries, sugar, and ¼ teaspoon of cinnamon in pie plate until well mixed. Combine oats, brown sugar, butter, flour, and the remaining cinnamon in mixing bowl; blend with fingertips until mixture is a coarse meal. Sprinkle oat mixture over fruit and pat down lightly. Bake until pears are tender and topping is golden, about 45 minutes. Serve warm with vanilla ice cream. **Serves 6.**

RHUBARB CRISP

INGREDIENTS:

3 cups diced rhubarb
¾ cup sugar
¼ cup water
½ cup (1 stick) butter or margarine
1 cup firmly packed brown sugar
1¼ cups all-purpose flour

EQUIPMENT:

2 medium (2½-quart) mixing bowls
8-inch square baking dish
Pastry blender

Preheat oven to 350°. Mix rhubarb, sugar, and water in a bowl and place in greased baking dish. In second bowl, cut butter into brown sugar and flour, using pastry blender, until mixture is crumbly. Spread crumbs over rhubarb and bake 40 minutes, or until crumb topping is lightly browned and rhubarb is tender. Serve warm or cold, plain, or with cream or ice cream. **Serves 4 to 6.**

ICED WINTER FRUIT

An elegantly simple dessert, perfect for a party.

INGREDIENTS:

2 to 3 large bunches of red grapes
About ¼ cup superfine sugar
4 tangerines or oranges, peeled and in segments
8 ounces bittersweet chocolate

EQUIPMENT:

Freezer storage container
Double boiler
Baking sheet

Leaving them in bunches, wash grapes. While still wet, sprinkle with sugar. Put in a freezer storage container and freeze at least 2 hours.

Melt the chocolate in double boiler over hot (not simmering) water. Use a toothpick to dip the orange segments in the chocolate. Place segments on baking sheet lined with wax paper and store, covered, in the refrigerator to harden.

Just before serving, place frozen grapes in the middle of a platter. Surround with chocolate-dipped orange segments. **Serves 6.**

TIP: You can microwave chocolate (in a glass bowl or measure) on HIGH for 30 seconds, stir, then continue at 30 second intervals until melted.

Iced Winter Fruit

DATE-NUT BARS

INGREDIENTS:

½ cup (1 stick) butter or margarine, softened
½ cup sugar
½ cup light molasses
1 egg
1 cup sifted all-purpose flour
½ teaspoon salt
¼ teaspoon cinnamon
½ teaspoon baking soda
¼ cup seedless raisins
8 ounces pitted dates, chopped
1 cup chopped pecans or walnuts
Frosting:
1 cup confectioner's sugar
3 tablespoons milk, hot
½ teaspoon cinnamon

EQUIPMENT:

Medium (2½-quart) mixing bowl
Small (1-quart) mixing bowl
8-inch square baking pan

Preheat oven to 350°. Cream together butter, sugar, and molasses in medium bowl; add egg and beat until light. Reserving 3 tablespoons of the flour, sift flour, salt, cinnamon, and baking soda together in small bowl, add to egg mixture and blend. Toss raisins and chopped dates with reserved flour in small bowl. Stir raisin-date mixture and ¾ cup of the nuts into batter. Bake in greased and floured pan for 35 minutes.

To make frosting, mix together confectioner's sugar, milk, and cinnamon in small bowl. While bars are still warm, spread with frosting and sprinkle with remaining ¼ cup nuts. Cool in pan, and cut into bars. **Yield: 36 bars.**

Citrus Cake

CITRUS CAKE

INGREDIENTS:
2 cups cake flour, sifted
2 teaspoons baking powder
¼ teaspoon salt
½ cup butter (1 stick) or margarine, softened
1 cup sugar
3 egg yolks
1 tablespoon finely grated orange rind
¾ cup milk
Frosting:
½ cup butter, (1 stick) softened
4 cups confectioners' sugar
2 tablespoons hot milk
Grated rind and strained juice of 1 lemon
Grated rind and strained juice of ½ orange

EQUIPMENT:
Small (1-quart) mixing bowl
Large (4-quart) mixing bowl
Electric mixer
2 8-inch cake pans
Food processor or blender

Preheat oven to 350°. Sift together flour, baking powder, and salt in small bowl. In large bowl, add sugar to softened butter, creaming until thoroughly blended. Beat in egg yolks and add orange rind; continue beating until mixture is light. Add half of flour mixture and half of milk to butter mixture, beating constantly at low speed. Continue beating while adding the remaining flour and milk.

Lightly grease and flour cake pans. Pour batter into pans and bake 30 minutes, or until a toothpick inserted in the center comes out clean. Allow to cool on rack before removing cakes from pans.

To make frosting, place softened butter in container of food processor. Add confectioners' sugar and process until thoroughly blended, adding hot milk a little at a time. Add grated rind and juice of lemon and orange; continue processing 2 minutes more.

To frost the cake: In general, cakes tend to rise more in the center than at the sides. Trim the layer you plan to use on the bottom so that it is perfectly flat before spreading it with about a third of the frosting. Place the second layer on top, then spread the remaining frosting over the top and sides.
Serves 6.

TIP: For a truly elegant dessert, spread raspberry preserves between the layers, then frost top and sides. Delicious!

149

CARROT CAKE

INGREDIENTS:
2 cups all-purpose flour
½ teaspoon salt
2 teaspoons baking powder
¼ teaspoon baking soda
½ teaspoon ground cinnamon
½ teaspoon ground nutmeg
¼ teaspoon ground cloves
½ teaspoon allspice
½ cup (1 stick) butter or margarine, softened
1 cup sugar
2 eggs
1 teaspoon vanilla extract
1 cup cooked, mashed carrots, about 6 medium carrots
½ cup milk
¾ cup raisins

Frosting:
3 ounces cream cheese or Neufchâtel
2 tablespoons unsalted butter
1 cup confectioner's sugar
¼ teaspoon vanilla extract
1 teaspoon fresh lemon juice

EQUIPMENT:
Small (1½-quart) mixing bowl
Medium (2½-quart) mixing bowl
8-inch square cake dish
Small (1½-quart) mixing bowl

Preheat oven to 350°. Combine flour, salt, baking powder, baking soda, and spices in small bowl. Cream butter and sugar in medium bowl until well blended. Add eggs, one at a time, beating well after each egg; add vanilla and mix well. Add carrots and mix well. Stir in dry ingredients one-half at a time, alternating with milk. Stir in raisins. Turn into greased baking pan and bake 45 to 50 minutes or until cake springs back when lightly touched near center. Cool in pan on rack. Frost when cool.

To make frosting, bring cream cheese and butter to room temperature; cream together in small bowl until smooth. Gradually beat in confectioner's sugar; blend in vanilla and lemon juice, mixing well. If frosting is too soft, add a little more sugar. If too stiff, blend in a small amount of milk. **Serves 6.**

GINGERBREAD CAKE

The absence of egg yolks, milk, or butter make this a non-cholesterol dessert.

INGREDIENTS:
⅓ cup vegetable oil
⅓ cup water
⅓ cup light molasses
⅓ cup sugar
2 egg whites, lightly beaten
1 cup all-purpose flour
¼ teaspoon salt
¼ teaspoon baking soda
1 teaspoon baking powder
1 tablespoon ground ginger
2 teaspoons ground cinnamon
½ teaspoon ground nutmeg

EQUIPMENT:
Small (1-quart) mixing bowl
Food processor or electric beater
8-inch square baking pan

Preheat oven to 350°. Combine oil, water, molasses, sugar, and egg whites. Stir until well mixed or use food processor. Mix flour, salt, baking soda, baking powder, and spices in a small bowl. Add to liquid mixture. Beat or combine in a food processor until smooth. Pour into greased baking pan. Bake 30 minutes or until surface springs back when touched lightly. **Serves 4 to 6.** ●

TIP: You can frost this cake with the icing used for Carrot Cake (see above) or Perfect Pumpkin Cake (see p. 152). Or sprinkle with confectioner's sugar.

See photo, p. 37.

Chocolate Torte with Raspberry Sauce

CHOCOLATE TORTE

This delicious dessert tastes somewhat like a brownie—but better. Because there is no flour, it is very moist and dense without feeling heavy. For chocolate lovers, this torte is sheer perfection.

INGREDIENTS:

5 ounces semisweet chocolate
10 tablespoons butter (we don't recommend margarine)
⅔ cup sugar
5 eggs, separated

EQUIPMENT:

1-quart saucepan
Large (4-quart) mixing bowl
Electric mixer
Medium (2½-quart) mixing bowl
9-inch round cake pan

TIP: Make sure the beaters are completely fat-free before beating egg whites. Even a drop of chocolate or egg yolk can prevent the whites from becoming stiff.

Preheat oven to 325°. Melt chocolate and butter together in saucepan over low heat, stirring occasionally. Remove saucepan from heat, add sugar, mix thoroughly, and allow to cool. Place egg yolks in large bowl, add chocolate mixture, and beat 10 to 15 minutes with electric mixer on high. In medium bowl, beat egg whites until stiff and gently fold into chocolate mixture with a spatula. Pour batter into well-greased and floured 9-inch cake pan. Bake 35 minutes or until torte rises and top is firm. It will still seem moist in center so a toothpick inserted in center won't be clean; it should still have some chocolate clinging to it.

Let torte cool in pan for 8 to 10 minutes; it will fall slightly. To remove from pan, carefully run a thin knife around the edge. Hold cake rack on top of pan and flip over; gently lift pan from torte. Holding a serving plate against torte, quickly flip over again so that the "rounded" side of torte is up. Allow torte to cool thoroughly before serving. It can be refrigerated for several days but return to room temperature before serving. Serve plain or sprinkle with confectioner's sugar—or decorate with fresh raspberries, candied orange peel, or chocolate shavings. **Serves 6.**

CHOCOLATE ANGEL-FOOD CAKE

This low-fat, low-cholesterol dessert is a perennial favorite. There is no fat at all if you make a plain angel-food cake by replacing the ¼ cup cocoa in this recipe with an additional ¼ cup cake flour.

INGREDIENTS:
1½ cups egg whites (about 10 eggs) at room temperature
1¼ teaspoons cream of tartar
¼ teaspoon salt
1 teaspoon vanilla extract
1¼ cups sugar
¾ cup cake flour
¼ cup cocoa

EQUIPMENT:
Large (4-quart) mixing bowl
Electric mixer
Small (1-quart) mixing bowl
10-inch nonstick tube pan

Combine egg whites, cream of tartar, salt, and vanilla in large bowl and beat with electric mixer until mixture holds peaks. Continue beating, adding ½ cup of the sugar a little at a time. In small bowl, blend flour, cocoa, and remaining sugar. Sift mixture on top of egg whites and gently fold in with a rubber spatula.

Spoon batter into tube pan and bake 30 to 40 minutes or until a toothpick inserted in center comes out clean. Remove from oven, immediately turn pan upside down on rack, but do not remove cake. When cool, remove cake and serve plain or with a melted chocolate glaze or Raspberry Sauce (see p. 154). **Serves 6.** ●

TIP: Because egg sizes vary significantly, add egg whites one at a time to measuring cup.

PERFECT PUMPKIN CAKE

INGREDIENTS:
3 cups all-purpose flour
1½ cups sugar
1¼ cups vegetable oil
3½ teaspoons ground cinnamon
2 teaspoons baking powder
1 teaspoon salt
4 eggs
1 (16-ounce) can pureed pumpkin (not pumpkin-pie filling)
1 cup walnuts, coarsely chopped (optional)

Frosting:
6 ounces cream cheese or Neufchâtel
1 teaspoon vanilla extract
Dash of salt
2 cups confectioner's sugar
3 teaspoons milk

EQUIPMENT:
Large (4-quart) mixing bowl
Electric mixer
Bundt pan
Medium (2½-quart) mixing bowl

Preheat oven to 350°. To make the cake, measure all ingredients except walnuts into large bowl. With electric mixer, beat at low speed until ingredients are just mixed. Then increase mixer speed to high and beat 5 minutes. Stir in walnuts by hand. Pour batter into greased bundt pan and bake 1 hour. Cool on a baking rack before removing from pan.

In medium bowl, combine cream cheese, vanilla, and salt; beat with electric mixer until smooth. Gradually add confectioner's sugar and mix until combined. Add milk one teaspoon at a time until it reaches desired consistency. Pour over cake evenly and let frosting set at least an hour before serving at room temperature. **Serves 6.**

Island Sherbet

ISLAND SHERBET

This sherbet is delicious served by itself or with kiwi fruit and mango, in keeping with the tropical-island theme.

INGREDIENTS:
¼ cup sugar
1 cup warm water
½ cup corn syrup
¼ cup fresh lime juice
8 large very ripe bananas
2 egg whites

EQUIPMENT:
Small (1-quart) mixing bowl
2 medium (2½-quart) mixing bowls
Food processor or blender

In small bowl, dissolve sugar in warm water. Add corn syrup and lime juice, stirring constantly. Transfer to food processor, add bananas, and puree. Remove to medium bowl. In another medium bowl, beat egg whites until stiff and fold into puree mixture. Freeze until firm. **Serves 6.**

BLUEBERRY SAUCE

Serve warm, at room temperature, or chilled over ice cream or pound cake.

INGREDIENTS:
2 teaspoons cornstarch
½ cup water
¾ cup fresh or frozen unsweetened blueberries, thawed, crushed
2 tablespoons honey
2 teaspoons fresh lemon juice

EQUIPMENT:
1-quart saucepan

Combine cornstarch with a small amount of the water in saucepan and stir until smooth. Add remaining water, blueberries, and honey. Bring to a boil over medium heat, stirring constantly. Reduce heat to low and cook until thickened. Remove from heat and stir in lemon juice. **Yield: about 1 cup.** ● ■

MICROWAVE DIRECTIONS: Mix cornstarch with 2 tablespoons of the cold water. Add remaining water, berries, and honey. Cook 3 minutes on HIGH, stirring after each minute. Add additional cooking time in 30-second increments (stirring each time) until mixture thickens. Stir in lemon juice.

RASPBERRY SAUCE

Try this sauce over ice cream, fresh peaches, pound cake, pears, or Chocolate Torte (see p. 151).

INGREDIENTS:
1 (10-ounce) package frozen raspberries in light syrup
1 teaspoon grated lemon rind
½ cup raspberry jam or currant jelly
1½ teaspoons cornstarch
1 tablespoon fresh lemon juice

EQUIPMENT:
1-quart glass or ceramic saucepan
Sieve
Small dish

See photo, p. 151.

Place raspberries in a nonreactive saucepan. Thaw over low heat on range top, or in microwave oven, breaking up raspberries occasionally as they thaw. Stir in lemon rind and jam. Bring to a boil over low heat and cook 6 to 8 minutes, stirring constantly, or in microwave oven 3 to 5 minutes on HIGH, stirring at 1-minute intervals.

Strain mixture through a sieve to remove seeds and rind. Return mixture to saucepan. Mix cornstarch and lemon juice in a small dish and add to the raspberries. Cook on low heat, stirring until mixture clears. Cool by refrigerating immediately in the same cooking pan. Stir frequently during cooling. **Yield: about 1 cup.** ●

BANANA "ICE CREAM"

INGREDIENTS:
6 bananas, sliced and frozen
1 teaspoon vanilla extract

EQUIPMENT:
Food processor or blender

Puree frozen bananas with vanilla extract in food processor until smooth. Serve in bowls with fresh sliced fruit, or pureed raspberries. **Serves 4.**
● ■

TIP: Turn this simple dessert into a gourmet specialty by substituting 1 to 2 tablespoons of Cointreau, Grand Marnier, or banana liqueur for the vanilla. You can also add 6 to 10 frozen strawberries in chunks—or blended with the bananas.

*Rice Pudding
with Fresh Fruit*

RICE PUDDING WITH FRESH FRUIT

INGREDIENTS:

4½ cups milk
⅔ cup long-grain white rice
2 tablespoons sugar
¼ teaspoon salt
2 eggs
1 teaspoon vanilla extract
¼ teaspoon ground cinnamon

Topping:

½ pint strawberries, hulled and thickly sliced
2 small bananas, sliced and sprinkled with lemon
   juice
1 large kiwi fruit, peeled and sliced
½ cup seedless red grapes, cut in half
Maple syrup (optional)

EQUIPMENT:

3-quart saucepan
Small (1-quart) mixing bowl

In saucepan over high heat, combine milk, rice, sugar, and salt and bring to a boil. Reduce heat to medium and cook, uncovered, 20 minutes or until rice is tender, stirring frequently.

In small bowl, beat eggs slightly with a fork; stir in small amount of hot rice mixture. Slowly pour egg mixture into rice in saucepan, stirring rapidly to prevent lumping. Cook over low heat, stirring, until rice mixture is slightly thickened, about 1 minute. Do not boil or mixture will curdle. Remove from heat; stir in vanilla extract and cinnamon. Serve pudding warm or refrigerate to serve cold later.

Just before serving, arrange fruit on top of rice pudding. Maple syrup to pour over each serving can be passed separately. **Serves 6.**

INDIAN PUDDING

INGREDIENTS:
½ cup yellow cornmeal
1 cup water
½ teaspoon salt
3 cups milk
1 egg, beaten
⅓ cup sugar
½ cup molasses
1 tablespoon butter or margarine
1 teaspoon ground cinnamon
½ teaspoon ground ginger

TIP: See p. 157 for *bain-marie* instructions.

EQUIPMENT:
3-quart saucepan
Small (1-quart) bowl
8-inch square baking pan
Deep roasting pan

Preheat oven to 325°. Mix cornmeal, water, salt, and 2 cups of the milk in a saucepan. Bring to a gentle boil and boil for 10 minutes while stirring. In bowl, mix egg, sugar, molasses, butter, and spices. Stir into cornmeal mixture. Pour into greased baking pan. Pour 1 cup milk over top. Bake in a *bain-marie* for 30 minutes. Stir if milk has not evaporated. Bake an additional 1½ hours. Serve warm or at room temperature with cream or ice cream. **Serves 6.**

DESSERT CREPES

Crepes are a versatile dessert that can be served with a variety of fillings. Try them simply with butter and powdered sugar; or heated jam of your choice, lemon or orange marmalade, or red currant jelly; or fresh fruit, sugar, and a liqueur. They are also good covered with a thin chocolate sauce or honey. To serve, spread with filling and roll.

INGREDIENTS:
2 cups all-purpose flour
2 cups milk
4 eggs
1 tablespoon melted butter, margarine, or
    vegetable oil
Pinch of salt
1 tablespoon sugar (optional)
½ teaspoon lemon zest (optional)

EQUIPMENT:
Food processor or blender
8-inch nonstick skillet

TIP: Crepes can be stored in the refrigerator for up to two days.

Put all ingredients in food processor in the order given and blend for about 1 minute. Batter should be smooth and thin. Into skillet over medium-high heat, pour approximately 3 tablespoons of batter to cover bottom of pan. Tilt pan so that batter spreads evenly. Cook 30 to 45 seconds; turn crepe and cook another 15 to 30 seconds. Crepes should be lightly brown. Keep them warm in a barely heated oven. Serve immediately with toppings suggested above. **Yield: 24 crepes.**

VARIATION—CREPE CAKE: Stack all the crepes one atop another, with a moist filling (see serving suggestions above) between each crepe. Sprinkle top with powdered sugar and melted butter. Top with 1 to 2 tablespoons of kirsch, cognac, Grand Marnier or any fruit liqueur. Heat in a 350° oven until warm. Serve immediately and slice as you would a cake. You can cook the crepes before dinner and reheat immediately before serving. However, don't assemble the cake more than 4 hours before serving. **Serves 4 to 6.**

Dessert Crepes

Royal Meringue with Berries

ROYAL MERINGUE WITH BERRIES

This is a most unusual meringue. It has a custardlike consistency
and is baked in a *bain marie*, or water bath.

INGREDIENTS:

10 egg whites
¾ teaspoon cream of tartar
1¼ cups sugar
Dash almond extract
2 pints fresh strawberries, raspberries, or the
    equivalent amount of chopped fresh peaches
    (you may substitute frozen fruit, well drained).
¼ teaspoon almond extract, or dark rum if using
    peaches
Sugar to taste

EQUIPMENT:

Large (4 quart) mixing bowl
Electric mixer
8-inch square baking pan
Deep roasting pan
Food processor or blender

Preheat oven to 300°. In bowl, beat egg whites
with cream of tartar until foamy. Slowly add sugar
and beat until very thick. Fold in almond extract
and spoon into baking pan. Bake in a *bain marie:* Set
in a larger pan and add hot water to come halfway up
the sides of the inner pan.

Bake 1 hour. Remove pan from water bath and
set on a rack to cool. Meringue will fall slightly as
it cools.

Place berries in food processor or blender. Add
a little sugar (or not, according to taste) plus almond
extract or rum. Pulse into a coarse puree. Spoon
meringue onto individual serving plates and top
with berry mixture. **Serves 6.** ●

VARIATION: If you don't mind the calories or fat,
fold 1 cup of lightly whipped cream into the berry
mixture.

STRAWBERRY TART

INGREDIENTS:
9-inch pastry crust (see p. 160)
Pastry cream:
3 large egg yolks
½ cup sugar
2 cups whole milk
3 tablespoons cornstarch
1 tablespoon unsalted butter
2 teaspoons vanilla extract
1 quart firm, ripe strawberries, hulled
½ cup currant jelly

EQUIPMENT:
9-inch pie plate
Medium (2½-quart) mixing bowl
2-quart saucepan
1-quart saucepan

TIP: Pastry cream will keep 3 or 4 days in the refrigerator; it also freezes well. If you plan on storing it for future use, spoon warm mixture into glass storage container and dot surface with unsalted butter. The butter will melt, coating the surface of the cream and preventing a skin from forming. Allow the pastry cream to cool, then cover container tightly and refrigerate or freeze.

VARIATIONS: Try an equivalent amount of other fresh fruits such as raspberries, grapes, sliced bananas, or kiwis, or poached pears, peaches, or apricots.
Try adding 1 to 2 tablespoons kirsch, cognac, Grand Marnier, or rum to the pastry cream.

Preheat oven to 400°. Press pastry dough into pie plate. Cover with parchment paper or aluminum foil and weight it down with a handful of dried beans. Bake 10 minutes, then remove paper or foil and beans; prick bottom of pastry shell with a fork in several places and return it to oven for 5 more minutes, or until edge of shell is light brown. Remove from oven and cool at room temperature before filling.

To make pastry cream, beat egg yolks and sugar in bowl with a wire whisk until thoroughly blended. In saucepan over medium heat, bring milk to just below the boiling point (or microwave 5 to 6 minutes in a small microwaveable bowl). While milk is heating, add cornstarch one teaspoon at a time to the egg-and-sugar mixture, whisking constantly to prevent lumps from forming. Remove milk from heat and pour *very slowly* into egg mixture, whisking until smooth. Return mixture to saucepan in which you heated the milk. Over medium heat, bring to a simmer, whisking vigorously. Continue simmering and whisking 2 to 3 minutes, or until mixture coats the back of a spoon. Remove from heat; stir in butter and vanilla and refrigerate.

Melt jelly over low heat in small saucepan. Using a pastry brush, paint the inside of the pastry shell with some of the melted jelly and let set for 5 minutes. Cover glazed bottom of pastry with 1¼ to 1½ cups pastry cream. Arrange fruit over pastry cream in an attractive pattern and glaze with remaining melted jelly. Refrigerate and serve at room temperature. **Serves 6.**

INSTANT, DELICIOUS DESSERTS:
•Strawberries, brown sugar, and sour cream. Dip whole strawberries in sour cream then brown sugar.
•Melon frappe: Process in blender four parts melon to one part lemon- or limeade; serve in a glass, garnish with fresh fruit or a scoop of sorbet.
•Mix equal parts sesame tahini and plain yogurt; blend with a little of your favorite jam.

Strawberry Tart

PEACH TART

INGREDIENTS:
Sweet pastry for one 9-inch pie crust:
1½ cups all-purpose flour
¼ cup superfine sugar
¼ teaspoon salt
½ cup (1 stick) unsalted butter, chilled
2 egg yolks, (reserve whites, see TIP)
2 tablespoons water
½ teaspoon vanilla extract
Filling:
8 to 10 firm ripe peaches
⅓ cup plus 2 tablespoons sugar
2 tablespoons butter or margarine
4 tablespoons apple jelly

EQUIPMENT:
Large (4-quart) mixing bowl
Pastry blender
Small (1-quart) mixing bowl
Rolling pin
9-inch pie plate
Small saucepan

Sift flour, sugar, and salt together in large bowl. Cut butter into small pieces and blend into dry ingredients using pastry blender, until mixture resembles coarse meal. In small bowl, mix egg yolks, water, and vanilla extract; add to flour mixture and blend with a fork. Form dough into a ball, wrap in wax paper, and chill in refrigerator for 45 minutes.

Roll out dough on a floured board or between two sheets of waxed paper into a circle ⅛-inch thick and slightly larger than pie pan. Line pie plate with pastry, press it into place lightly with your fingers, and trim off excess around the rim. Chill in refrigerator at least 20 minutes before filling.

Preheat oven to 375°. Peel fruit, cut in half, pit, and slice. Sprinkle pastry shell with 3 tablespoons sugar. Arrange slices of fruit in circles of overlapping layers. Sprinkle remaining sugar over fruit and dot with butter. Bake 35 to 40 minutes. Remove tart from oven. Melt apple jelly in small saucepan and pour over fruit while still warm from oven. Allow tart to cool to room temperature before serving. **Serves 6.**

TIP: Before filling, brush pastry with beaten egg white to prevent sogginess.

POACHED PEARS

Serve with Curried Cookies (see p. 146) and a dessert cheese.

INGREDIENTS:
4 firm ripe pears, peeled, cored (from the bottom), stems intact
3 tablespoons fresh lemon juice
1 small strip lemon rind
½ teaspoon ground cloves
½ cup sugar
½ cup red wine or cranberry juice

EQUIPMENT:
2-quart covered saucepan

Brush pears with lemon juice and set aside. In saucepan, place remaining juice and all other ingredients. Cook over high heat 1 minute, then stir and cook an additional minute or until sugar is dissolved. Stand pears in the mixture and baste them with the sauce. A bulb baster does this job well. Cover and simmer 12 minutes, basting every 3 minutes. Test for doneness; pears should be tender enough to be easily pierced with a fork. Let pears cool in their liquid, basting occasionally. Serve chilled or at room temperature. Nutmeg-laced whipped cream or plain yogurt can be served on the side. **Serves 4.** ●

Baked Eggs Italiano and *English Scones*

VALENTINE'S DAY
BREAKFAST IN BED

Cold Fruit Soup
Baked Eggs Italiano
English Scones and Strawberry or Raspberry Jam
Banana "Ice Cream" with Sliced Fresh Strawberries

Start your Valentine's Day with this delicious breakfast in bed, and it just might become a tradition. Prepare the *Cold Fruit Soup* (see p. 40), *English Scones* (see p. 137), and *Banana "Ice Cream"* (see p. 154) the day before. Then 15 to 20 minutes in the kitchen on Valentine's morning will be all you'll need to prepare this treat for your loved one.

You can even assemble the *Baked Eggs Italiano* (see p. 139) the night before. Prepare the recipe up to the point where you add the eggs. Cover tightly with plastic wrap and refrigerate.

Bed serving trays are essential; paper or lace doilies add an appropriate Valentine's Day touch. Use your best china, cutlery, glassware, and cloth napkins. Tie white napkins with crimson ribbons or use red or pink napkins. And don't forget a bud vase with a long-stemmed rose along with your Valentine's card or gift.

FAST AND FABULOUS

On days when your inspiration seems to fizzle out or time is precious, it can be helpful to have a preplanned, simple menu to follow. With the following seven dinners you'll spend only thirty minutes in the kitchen and present a gourmet meal fit for a dinner party. Each menu is designed to serve four.

THE MEAL

Spaghetti Squash al Fresco
Italian Bread
Green Salad with Garlic Vinaigrette

Serve spaghetti squash with Italian bread and a tossed green salad of romaine and watercress or bibb lettuce with Garlic Vinaigrette (see p. 30). You don't have to eat it outdoors, but you *should* use the freshest ingredients available.

SPAGHETTI SQUASH AL FRESCO

INGREDIENTS:
1 spaghetti squash, about 2 pounds, quartered
3 cups water
Pinch of salt
2 tablespoons olive oil
2 garlic cloves, minced
6 scallions, white and tender greens, chopped
2 small carrots, scrubbed and cut into ½-inch rounds
1 small green bell pepper, seeded, cored, and sliced into thin strips
2 small zucchini, cut into ½-inch rounds
½ cup dry white wine
6 fresh basil leaves, chopped, or 1 teaspoon dried sweet basil
8 cherry tomatoes, halved
Salt and freshly ground black pepper to taste
¼ to ½ cup freshly grated Parmesan cheese (optional)

EQUIPMENT:
6-quart covered stockpot
10-inch covered sauté pan

Remove seeds and fiber from squash. Bring salted water to a boil in stockpot, add squash, cover, and boil for 15 to 20 minutes, or until flesh of squash is tender.

While squash is cooking, heat oil in sauté pan over medium heat. Add garlic and scallions and stir-fry 1 minute. Add carrots, pepper, and zucchini; sauté, stirring constantly, 5 minutes. Add white wine and basil. Cover, lower heat, and simmer 10 minutes. Add cherry tomatoes, season with salt and pepper, and simmer uncovered 2 minutes more. Remove from heat immediately to avoid overcooking.

Drain squash and set aside until cool enough to handle. Scrape out the spaghettilike strands of flesh and form into "nests" on four dinner plates. Mound equal amounts of vegetable mixture in the center of each nest. Serve grated Parmesan cheese on the side, if desired. **Serves 4.** ▼ ● ■

Spaghetti Squash Al Fresco

Chicken with Tarragon and *Green Beans with Hot Vinaigrette*

THE MEAL

Chicken with Tarragon
Green Beans with Hot Vinaigrette
Sliced Tomatoes and Basil

Serve chicken and green beans with a simple tomato salad of sliced tomatoes drizzled with oil and chopped fresh basil, salt, and pepper.

CHICKEN WITH TARRAGON

INGREDIENTS:
2 whole chicken breasts, skinned, boned, and cut in half
4 teaspoons dried tarragon
Salt and freshly ground black pepper to taste
3 tablespoons butter *or* 1 tablespoon butter and 2 tablespoons vegetable oil
⅔ cup dry white wine

EQUIPMENT:
10-inch covered skillet

Sprinkle chicken breasts with tarragon, salt, and pepper. Melt butter in skillet over medium heat and sauté chicken 3 to 4 minutes on each side until lightly browned. Add wine, cover, and simmer over low heat 15 to 20 minutes or until chicken is cooked through. **Serves 4.**

GREEN BEANS WITH HOT VINAIGRETTE

Add green beans to steamer when chicken begins simmering.

INGREDIENTS:
1 pound green beans
3 tablespoons olive oil
3 tablespoons tarragon vinegar
1 teaspoon grated onion
Salt and freshly ground black pepper to taste

EQUIPMENT:
2-quart covered saucepan with steamer
1-quart saucepan

Steam or boil green beans 5 to 10 minutes or until tender-crisp. Combine remaining ingredients in small saucepan. Bring to a boil and remove from heat; pour over green beans and serve. **Serves 4.**

Baja Tacos

THE MEAL

Baja Tacos
Steamed Zucchini with Tomatoes

BAJA TACOS

INGREDIENTS:
1 package corn tortillas, preferably blue corn
1 pound lean ground beef
2 tablespoons red-wine vinegar
4 to 6 scallions, white and tender greens,
  chopped
1 teaspoon ground cumin
2 tablespoons chili powder
1 (8-ounce) can tomato sauce
2 drops hot pepper sauce
Salt and cayenne pepper to taste

Toppings:
Chopped tomatoes, salsa, grated cheddar cheese,
avocado slices, sour cream, chopped fresh cilantro
leaves, fresh watercress or arugula

EQUIPMENT:
10-inch skillet

Preheat oven to 350°. Wrap tortillas in aluminum foil and warm in oven while meal is prepared. Heat skillet over medium-high heat, add beef, and brown. Drain fat and add remaining ingredients. Stir and cook 15 to 20 minutes over medium heat.

Serve with tortillas and generous amounts of toppings on the side; let everyone assemble his or her own tacos. **Serves 4.**

TIP: You can also blend the cooked beef with chopped tomato and/or salsa "garnish" to simplify the assembly of tacos.

STEAMED ZUCCHINI WITH TOMATOES

While beef is cooking, prepare this steamed-vegetable dish.

INGREDIENTS:

3 small zucchini, thinly sliced
1 pint cherry tomatoes, stems removed
1 tablespoon olive oil
1 to 2 teaspoons dried marjoram
Salt and freshly ground black pepper to taste

EQUIPMENT:

2-quart covered saucepan with steamer

Bring water to a boil in saucepan, place zucchini in steamer and steam for 3 to 4 minutes until tender-crisp. Add tomatoes and steam for an additional minute or until tomatoes are warm. Remove to a serving bowl; toss with olive oil and marjoram, salt and pepper. **Serves 4.** ● ■

Angel-Hair Pasta and Artichokes and *Green Salad*

THE MEAL

Angel-Hair Pasta and Artichokes
Herbed Bread with Tomatoes
Green Salad with Dijon Vinaigrette

Serve pasta and bread with tossed green salad—a simple salad of arugula or romaine with bibb lettuce and Dijon Vinaigrette (see p. 30) would be ideal.

HERBED BREAD WITH TOMATOES

INGREDIENTS:
1 large tomato, thinly sliced
1 loaf crusty Italian bread
1 tablespoon plus 1 teaspoon olive oil
2 tablespoons finely chopped fresh basil leaves or
    2 teaspoons dried sweet basil
2 teaspoons dried oregano or marjoram
2 to 3 tablespoons grated Parmesan cheese

Preheat oven to 350°. Slice tomatoes and set aside. Slice bread in half lengthwise. Drizzle 1 tablespoon olive oil and half the herbs over both halves of bread. Wrap loaf in foil and heat in oven 10 minutes. Remove from oven and layer each half with sliced tomatoes; sprinkle with remaining herbs, oil, and Parmesan cheese. Place under broiler until bread is lightly browned. **Serves 4.**

ANGEL-HAIR PASTA AND ARTICHOKES
Begin preparing as soon as you've placed bread in oven.

INGREDIENTS:
1 pound angel-hair pasta
2 (10-ounce) packages frozen artichoke hearts,
    thawed
4 tablespoons olive oil
¼ cup grated Parmesan cheese
2 tablespoons chopped fresh marjoram leaves or 2
    teaspoons dried marjoram
2 garlic cloves, quartered
¼ cup sliced scallions, white and tender greens
1 generous squeeze fresh lemon juice
Salt and freshly ground black pepper to taste

EQUIPMENT:
6-quart stockpot
Food processor or blender
10-inch sauté pan

Prepare pasta in stockpot according to package directions. In food processor, puree thoroughly two-thirds of the artichokes, 3 tablespoons of the oil, Parmesan cheese, marjoram, garlic, and scallions. Coarsely chop remaining artichokes and squeeze lemon juice over them. Heat remaining tablespoon of oil in sauté pan over medium-high heat; add chopped artichokes and sauté 6 to 8 minutes or until tender. Add artichoke puree to pan and cook over medium heat until heated through. Season with salt and pepper to taste. Toss with pasta. **Serves 4.** ▼

THE MEAL

Lemon-Rosemary Chicken in Foil
Fettucini Classico
Steamed Spinach

LEMON-ROSEMARY CHICKEN IN FOIL

INGREDIENTS:

2 whole chicken breasts, rinsed, skinned, boned,
  and cut in half
2 lemons
2 teaspoons dried rosemary
2 scallions, white and tender greens, chopped
1 tablespoon butter or vegetable oil
1 large carrot, peeled and julienned

EQUIPMENT:

Shallow roasting pan

Preheat oven to 375°. Place each chicken breast on large square of foil. Cut one lemon in 4 wedges for squeezing juice, the other in thin slices. Squeeze lemon juice over each breast. Sprinkle each with herbs and scallions. Cover with butter and lemon slices and place julienned carrots on top. Seal foil tightly and place in pan. Bake for 25 to 30 minutes. Remove from foil, discard lemon slices and serve with carrots on top. **Serves 4.** ● ■

Lemon-Rosemary Chicken in Foil and *Fettucini Classico*

STEAMED SPINACH

INGREDIENTS:

3 pounds spinach
Butter or vinegar to taste
Salt and freshly ground black pepper to taste

EQUIPMENT:

3-quart covered saucepan

Place spinach leaves with water clinging to them in covered saucepan and cook for 5 to 10 minutes over medium-low heat. Serve with butter or vinegar, salt and pepper. **Serves 4.** ● ■

FETTUCINI CLASSICO

INGREDIENTS:

½ pound fettucini
2 tablespoons butter or margarine
4 tablespoons light cream
¼ cup grated Parmesan cheese
Salt and freshly ground black pepper to taste

EQUIPMENT:

3-quart saucepan

Cook pasta in saucepan according to package directions; drain and toss with remaining ingredients, and serve. **Serves 4.**

Peppers and Steak and *New Cottage Potatoes*

THE MEAL

Peppers and Steak
New Cottage Potatoes
Orange and Green Salad

PEPPERS AND STEAK

Serve on lettuce boats, Boston or bibb lettuce; flour tortillas, or crusty sandwich rolls.

INGREDIENTS:
4 tablespoons olive oil
2 shallots, sliced
2 small red, green, or yellow bell peppers,
    seeded, cored, and sliced
2 to 3 cherry peppers or equivalent amount of
    hot pepper, seeded and sliced
1 garlic clove, mashed
2 tablespoons red-wine vinegar
2 to 3 skirt steaks, about 4 to 5 ounces each
Salt and freshly ground black pepper to taste

EQUIPMENT:
10-inch skillet

Heat 3 tablespoons oil in skillet over medium-high heat. Add shallots, peppers, garlic, and vinegar. Sauté 10 minutes. Remove peppers from skillet; drain if necessary and set aside in warm oven. Drain skillet and wipe clean. Heat remaining tablespoon of olive oil in skillet over high heat. Add steaks, cooking about 3 minutes on each side; they will still be red in the center. Remove steaks and slice at an angle across the grain into thin strips. Combine with peppers and season with salt and pepper. **Serves 4.**

ORANGE AND GREEN SALAD

INGREDIENTS:

1 long seedless cucumber
1 orange, segments cut in chunks
2 tablespoons chopped fresh mint or 1 teaspoon
   dried mint
2 tablespoons vegetable oil
1 tablespoon wine or cider vinegar
Salt and freshly ground black pepper to taste

EQUIPMENT:

Small bowl or 2-cup measuring cup

    Slice cucumber, toss with orange and mint. Combine oil and vinegar; and drizzle over cucumber and oranges. Season with salt and pepper. **Serves 4.**

NEW COTTAGE POTATOES

INGREDIENTS:

12 to 16 small new potatoes
½ cup cottage cheese
Salt and paprika to taste

EQUIPMENT:

3-quart saucepan

    Bring water to boil in saucepan. Add potatoes and boil, uncovered, for 10 to 15 minutes or until tender. Drain and place in serving bowl. Mash potatoes with large fork, add cottage cheese, salt, and paprika. Blend with fork and serve. Mixture should be chunky, not smooth. **Serves 4.**

Salmon and Spinach with *Steamed Snow Peas*

THE MEAL

Salmon and Spinach
White Gazpacho
Steamed Snow Peas

SALMON AND SPINACH

INGREDIENTS:
2 tablespoons butter or margarine
1½ pounds fresh spinach
3 shallots, chopped
4 salmon fillets, about 5 ounces each
2 tablespoons fresh lemon juice
Salt and freshly ground black pepper to taste
1½ teaspoons chopped fresh rosemary leaves or ½
   teaspoon dried rosemary

EQUIPMENT:
3-quart shallow covered casserole

Preheat oven to 350°. Heavily grease casserole with butter or oil. Spread spinach leaves evenly over the bottom and sprinkle with shallots. Place salmon on spinach, skin-side down. Pour lemon juice over salmon and sprinkle with salt, pepper, and rosemary. Cover and bake 10 minutes. Remove lid and bake 5 to 10 minutes longer, or until flesh is opaque and salmon flakes when pierced with a fork. **Serves 4.** ● ■

WHITE GAZPACHO
Begin preparing after placing salmon in the oven.

INGREDIENTS:
2 cucumbers, peeled, seeded, and cut in 1-inch
   chunks
2 cups chicken broth, canned or homemade
1 garlic clove, quartered
¼ cup chopped scallions, white and tender
   greens
2 cups plain yogurt
2 tablespoons white-wine vinegar
4 tablespoons or more chopped fresh dill
2 fresh tomatoes, chopped, for garnish

EQUIPMENT:
Food processor or blender

Place cucumbers, 1 cup of the chicken broth, garlic, and scallions in food processor. Process to desired consistency. Remove to serving bowl and blend well with yogurt, vinegar, 2 tablespoons of the dill, and remaining chicken broth. Top each serving with chopped tomatoes and a generous helping of fresh dill. **Serves 4.** ● ■

STEAMED SNOW PEAS

INGREDIENTS:
¾ pound snow peas
1 tablespoon light sesame or vegetable oil
Salt and freshly ground black pepper to taste

EQUIPMENT:
2-quart covered saucepan with steamer

Place snow peas in steamer over boiling water and cook until crisp-tender, 1 to 2 minutes. Toss with oil, salt, and pepper. **Serves 4.** ● ■

THE KNOWLEDGEABLE COOK

One of the great pleasures of cooking comes from making a dish just the way *you* like it. Many recipes are "flexible." You can use more or less seasoning to suit your taste. Substitute or add favorite herbs or spices to create your own special version of a soup, stew, marinade, dressing, or main dish.

Many of the foods you eat can be chosen and prepared with good health in mind, too. It's easy when you know how.

FAT AND CHOLESTEROL

Watching your intake of fat and cholesterol is one of the best ways to establish healthier eating habits.

- A low-cholesterol diet can help fight heart disease.
- A low-fat diet is perhaps even more important in fighting heart disease and can help prevent certain cancers, diabetes, and other serious illnesses as well.

Although fat and cholesterol are often found in the same foods, they're not the same thing. However, dietary fat which comes from the foods we eat does have an impact on cholesterol levels, so it's important to limit the amounts of both in your diet.

Cholesterol, a white, waxy, fatlike substance, is contained in many of the foods we eat. Our bodies manufacture it, too. Dietary cholesterol (the cholesterol in foods) comes only from animal sources. Vegetables, fruits, and grains are cholesterol free. Serum, or blood, cholesterol is manufactured by our bodies and circulates in the human bloodstream. Its level is determined by many factors, including genetic background and foods consumed.

Serum cholesterol has two forms: LDL, or low-density lipoprotein; and HDL, or high-density lipoprotein. LDL—or "bad cholesterol"—is the cholesterol that clings to artery walls, clogging them. HDL—"good cholesterol"—transports cholesterol through your bloodstream to your liver, where it is broken down and then removed from your body. (Lipoproteins are protein "wrappers" that carry cholesterol through the blood.)

Cholesterol level can be controlled by the amount of cholesterol-rich foods in one's diet. The American Heart Association (AHA) recommends limiting daily dietary cholesterol to 100 milligrams for each 1,000 calories, with a maximum daily intake of 300 milligrams of cholesterol.

Fat is a food that provides calories (lots of them—9 per gram). It is visible on some foods—you can see it on uncooked meat, for example. In others, like many frozen prepared foods, it's hidden. Some foods, like butter or olive oil, are all fat. Generally speaking, oils, many meats, and certain dairy products contain the most fat; fruits, vegetables and grains are almost always fat free.

Controlling fat intake is an excellent way to keep cholesterol at desired levels. A high-fat diet can lead to any of several serious illnesses. The American Heart Association (AHA) recommends limiting fats to 30 percent of the total calories consumed in a day.

Dietary fats ("fatty acids") are classified as "saturated," "polyunsaturated," or "monounsaturated." All fats are actually combinations of the three, but because one fat is almost always dominant, fatty foods are classified according to their dominant fat. Because they influence health in different ways, it's good to be able to identify these fats.

Saturated fat is solid at room temperature—like a stick of butter or the fat that you can trim off a steak. It's generally found in animal products (e.g., meat and dairy foods). "Tropical oils" (coconut, palm-kernel, and palm oil) are high in saturated fat. Studies show that saturated fats raise blood levels of both LDL ("bad") and HDL ("good") cholesterol. The AHA recommends limiting saturated fats to less than one-third of your total fat intake.

Polyunsaturated fats (found in corn, safflower, cottonseed, and sunflower oils) stay liquid at room temperature or when refrigerated. They have been shown to reduce both LDL and HDL cholesterol. However, certain polyunsaturated fats may be linked to other health hazards. The AHA recommends limiting "polys" to less than one-third of your fat intake.

Italian Bread with Olive Oil and Herbs, see p. 138.

Monounsaturated fat is liquid at room temperature but solidifies when refrigerated. Olive, canola, walnut, and sesame oils are good examples of monounsaturated fats. These have been shown to lower only LDL blood cholesterol. The AHA recommends that "monos" be *more* than one-third of your total fat intake.

OMEGA-3 FATTY ACIDS

"Omega-3" fatty acids are polyunsaturated fats found in certain cold-water, fatty fish. Among their potential benefits is the fact that they may help prevent blood clots that cause heart attacks and may lower cholesterol and blood pressure. Fish high in Omega-3 fatty acids include:

Salmon	Mackerel	Herring	Trout	Tuna	Atlantic Halibut
Coho	Atlantic	Atlantic	Rainbow	Albacore	Sardines
Pink	Pacific	Pacific	Lake	Sockeye	Eel
King					
Atlantic					

Fat and Cholesterol Content of Meats, Poultry and Fish

The chart below gives information for 3 ounces of cooked foods.

MEAT:	Fat (grams)	Cholesterol (milligrams)
Beef		
Top round	5.4	84
Flank, lean	7.3	90
T-Bone steak, lean	10.4	80
Ground, lean	17.6	101
Chuck roast	24.4	99
Lamb, leg, lean	7.0	93
Pork		
Tenderloin, lean	4.8	93
Loin, top	14.9	94
Bacon (2 slices)	9.0	15
Veal, rump and round	11.2	101
POULTRY:		
Chicken		
White meat, skinless	3.6	85
White meat, with skin	10.9	85
Dark meat, skinless	9.7	93
Dark meat, with skin	15.8	93
Turkey		
White meat, skinless	3.2	69
White meat, with skin	8.3	76
Dark meat, skinless	7.2	85
Dark meat, with skin	11.5	89
FISH:		
Cod	0.9	55
Flounder	1.0	46
Haddock	0.9	74

	Fat (grams)	Cholesterol (milligrams)
Red Snapper	1.7	47
Salmon	11.0	87
Sole	0.8	42
Swordfish	5.1	50
Trout	4.3	74
Tuna		
Bluefin	6.2	49
White meat, water packed	2.5	42
SHELLFISH:		
Clams	2.0	67
Crabs	1.5	53
Lobster	0.6	72
Mussels	4.5	56
Oysters	2.2	50
Scallops	1.4	56
Shrimp	1.1	133

(Source: U.S. Department of Agriculture: *Bowes and Church's Food Values of Portions Commonly Used.*)

DAIRY PRODUCTS

Dairy products, although rich in bone-building calcium, are often high in fat and cholesterol. However, many delicious, healthful lower-fat alternatives are available in today's supermarkets. Fat and cholesterol content varies by brand; check labels before buying.

Fat and Cholesterol Content of Dairy Products

Product	Serving Size	Fat (grams)	Cholesterol (milligrams)
Milk			
Whole (4% milkfat)	8 oz.	8.0	34
Low-fat (2% milkfat)	8 oz	5.0	18
Low-fat (1% milkfat)	8 oz.	2.0	10
Skim (0% milkfat)	8 oz.	0.5	4
Buttermilk (low-fat)	8 oz.	2.2	9
Evaporated whole	1 oz.	2.4	9
Evaporated skim	1 oz.	0.1	1
Cream			
Heavy	1 T.	5.6	21
Medium	1 T.	3.8	13
Light	1 T.	2.9	10
Half & Half	1 T.	1.7	6
Yogurt			
Whole milk	8 oz.	6.0	20
Low-fat	8 oz.	3.0	14
Nonfat	8 oz.	0.0	5

Product	Serving Size	Fat (grams)	Cholesterol (milligrams)
Sour Cream			
Regular	1 T.	3.0	5
Light	1 T.	2.0	5
Substitute, Non-butterfat	1 T.	1.5	0
Substitute, Nonfat	1 T.	0.0	0
Cheese			
Cheddar			
Regular	1 oz.	9.0	30
Reduced fat	1 oz.	5.0	20
Cottage Cheese			
Creamed	4 oz.	5.0	17
Low-fat (2%)	4 oz.	3.0	10
Low-fat (1%)	4 oz.	1.0	15
Nonfat	4 oz.	0.0	0
Cream Cheese			
Regular	1 oz.	10.0	30
Light (Neufchâtel)	1 oz.	6.0	20
Muenster			
Regular	1 oz.	8.0	25
Low cholesterol	1 oz.	7.0	6
Mozzarella			
Whole milk	1 oz.	6.0	20
Part skim	1 oz.	3.0	10
Fat-free	1 oz.	0.0	5
Ricotta			
Whole milk	1 oz.	4.0	15
Part skim	1 oz.	3.0	10
Light	1 oz.	2.0	5
Fat-free	1 oz.	0.0	0
Butter			
Regular	1 t.	4.0	11
Light	1 t.	3.0	5
Margarine			
Regular	1 t.	4.0	0
Diet	1 t.	2.0	0
Butter/Margarine Blend	1 t.	3.0	3
Mayonnaise*			
Regular	1 T.	11.0	5
Light	1 T.	5.0	5
Reduced cholesterol	1 T.	5.0	0
Nonfat	1 T.	0.0	0

*Mayonnaise is not a dairy food, but is included for sake of comparison with other foods which can be substituted for it.

THE VIRTUES OF FRUITS AND VEGETABLES

Fruits and vegetables are important for a well-balanced diet. However, increasing your daily intake of fruits and vegetables can do more than provide essential nutrients—it may help prevent cancer and heart disease as well.

Fruits and vegetables are decidedly virtuous foods: most (avocadoes, olives, and coconuts being the exceptions) are fat free. They're rich in vitamins, minerals, and fiber and low in calories. That makes them a real nutritional bargain. At least four varied servings a day will meet minimum vitamin and mineral requirements. Just be sure to choose from among the following to meet these important needs:

Vitamin C

Broccoli
Brussels sprouts
Dark green, leafy vegetables
Grapefruit
Melons
Oranges

Pineapples
Potatoes
Red bell peppers
Strawberries
Tomatoes

Vitamin A

Apricots
Beets
Blueberries
Broccoli
Cantaloupe
Carrots
Corn
Dark green, leafy vegetables
Mangoes

Oranges
Peaches
Pink Grapefruit
Plums
Pumpkin
Sweet potatoes
Tangerines
Yams
Yellow squash

Calcium

Asparagus
Broccoli
Cauliflower

Dark green, leafy vegetables
Figs
Limas

Potassium

Apricots
Avocados
Bananas
Beets
Black raspberries
Broccoli
Cauliflower
Corn
Damson plums
Melons

Mushrooms
Oranges
Parsnips
Peaches
Potatoes
Pumpkin
Rhubarb
Spinach
Sweet potatoes
Tomatoes
Yams

Iron

Dark green, leafy vegetables
Dates
Dried apricots
Dried figs
Green peas

Jerusalem artichokes
Limas
Prunes
Raisins
Spinach

Fruits and vegetables also contain large amounts of fiber. Soluble fiber, the kind that dissolves in water, is found in many fruits and vegetables and in barley and oats. Soluble fiber helps lower blood cholesterol and thus helps prevent heart disease. Vegetables and fruits are also good sources of insoluble fiber, which does not dissolve in water. Bran and whole grains are other good sources. Insoluble fiber is a natural laxative and can help prevent colon cancer.

Choose from the following for a fiber boost:

Apples	Carrots	Figs	Mangos	Raspberries
Beets	Cauliflower	Grapes	Peppers	Rhubarb
Broccoli	Corn	Kale	Prunes	Spinach
Brussels Sprouts	Dates	Lettuce	Raisins	Strawberries
Cabbage	Eggplant			

SUBSTITUTIONS
FOR THE PANIC-PROOF CHEF

1 teaspoon baking powder	¼ teaspoon baking soda plus ½ teaspoon cream of tartar
1 cup buttermilk	1 cup plain yogurt OR 1 tablespoon lemon juice or cider vinegar, plus milk to equal 1 cup. Let stand 5 minutes.
1 cup sour cream	1 cup cottage cheese plus ⅛ cup yogurt OR 1 cup buttermilk mixed in blender OR 1 cup yogurt plus 1 tablespoon vinegar
1 cup plain yogurt	1 cup buttermilk
1 ounce semisweet chocolate	1 ounce unsweetened chocolate plus 1 tablespoon sugar
1 ounce unsweetened chocolate	3 tablespoons cocoa plus 1 tablespoon butter, margarine, or shortening
1 tablespoon cornstarch as thickener	2 tablespoons flour or 2 teaspoons arrowroot
1 teaspoon lemon juice	½ teaspoon vinegar
1 tablespoon dry mustard	1 tablespoon prepared mustard
1 tablespoon tapioca	1½ tablespoons all-purpose flour
1 cup tomato juice	½ cup tomato sauce plus ½ cup water
1 cup white wine	1 cup apple juice or cider

LEVEL MEASURE	EQUIVALENT
1 gallon	4 quarts
1 quart	4 cups 2 pints
1 cup	8 ounces ½ pint 16 tablespoons
2 tablespoons	1 ounce
1 tablespoon	3 teaspoons
1 pinch	less than ⅛ teaspoon (dry)
1 dash	¼ teaspoon (liquid)
1 pound	1 pint 16 ounces
1 pound regular butter or margarine	4 sticks 2 cups
1 pound *whipped* butter or margarine	6 sticks 2 (8-ounce) containers 3 cups

EQUIVALENT AMOUNTS

1 cup uncooked rice	3 cups cooked
1 cup dry beans	2½ cups cooked
1 pound regular butter or margarine	2 cups
1 pound uncooked spinach	About ¾ cup cooked
1 pound granulated sugar	2 cups
1 pound brown sugar	2¼ cups
1 pound confectioner's sugar	3½ cups
1 pound all-purpose flour	4½ cups, sifted
1 pound cheese	4½ cups, grated
1 square chocolate	1 ounce
1 pound cocoa	4 cups
1 pound macaroni	10 cups cooked
1 pound uncooked spaghetti	8 cups cooked
1 medium onion	½ cup chopped
1 pound raisins, seedless	3¼ cups

Index

184

Photo Credits

Page IV. Revere-Pro Line™ 4-Quart Dutch Oven; PYREX® 2½-Quart Bowl—Granite™

Page 4. 1. PYREX® Measuring Cups (1-Cup, 1-Pint, and 1-Quart)
2. REVERE® 3-Piece Mixing Bowl Set (1-, 2-, and 3-Quart Bowls with Plastic Covers)
3. PYREX® Storage Bowls (2-, 4-, and 7-Cup Bowls with Plastic Covers)
4. REVERE® 3½-Quart Colander
5. VISIONS® 5-Quart Dutch Oven
6. REVERE® Copper Clad 10-Quart Stockpot
7. REVERE® Spectrum™ 2-Quart Non-Stick Saucepan with Double Pourspout—Sapphire Blue™
8. VISIONS® 1½-Quart Double Boiler
9. REVERE® Aluminum Disc 2-Quart Saucepan REVERE® 2-Quart Steamer/Colander Inset
10. Cranberry™ VISIONS® 10″ Non-Stick Skillet
11. REVERE® Spectrum™ 8¼″ Non-Stick Saute Pan—Cabernet Red™
12. Revere-Pro Line™ 12″ Covered Sautoir
13. Revere-Pro Line™ 10″ Covered Au Gratin
14. REVERE® 15¼″ × 10½″ Cookie Sheet
15. REVERE® 6 Compartment Muffin Pan

Page 5. 16. PYREX® 9″ Pie Plate
17. REVERE® 9″ Round Cake Pan
18. CORNING WARE® CLASSIC BLACK® Quiche Dish
19. PYREX® 1½-Quart Loaf Dish
20. Sculptured™ PYREX® 3-Quart Baking Dish
21. CORNING WARE® 4-Quart Roaster—Symphony™
22. CORNING WARE® FRENCH WHITE® 4½-Quart Lasagna Dish
23. Cranberry™ VISIONS® 1½-Quart Casserole
24. PYREX® Custard Cups
25. CORNING WARE® FRENCH WHITE® 16-Oz. Round Casseroles

Page 12. PYREX® Storage 4-Cup Round Bowl; PYREX® 12″ Pizza Plate

Page 15. CORELLE® Impressions™ 12½″ Platter—Windward White™
Place mat: La Serviette/Gallery 339; Napkin: James Crow & Co.

Page 17. Prego™ Villa™ 10¾″ Dinner Plate—Plum Tablecloth/Napkin: James Crow & Co.

Page 18. CORNING WARE® CLASSIC BLACK® 24-Oz. Divided Dish with Serving Cradle; CORELLE® 12½″ Serving Platter—White

Page 20. CROWN CORNING® Duchess™ Chip & Dip Tablecloth: James Crow & Co.

Page 21. CORELLE® CORNERSTONE® 1-Quart Serving Bowl—Symphony™

Page 22. PYREX® 4-Quart Serving Bowl—White Burgundy napkin: La Serviette/Gallery 339

Page 25. Sculptured™ PYREX® 6-Cup Serving Bowl Tablecloth: James Crow & Co.

Page 27. Prego™ 7½″ Salad Plate—Hunter Green Gold/green napkins: W. C. Imports

Page 29. Prego™ Villa™ 12″ Round Platter—Burgundy™

Page 30. CORNING WARE® 2-Quart Covered Casserole—Forever Yours™

Page 31. CORELLE® OCCASIONS® 7¼″ Salad Plate—Silk and Roses™
Solid napkin: W. C. Imports

Page 32. Prego™ 20-Oz. Soup Bowl—Cobalt; Prego™ 7½″ Salad Plate—White; Prego™ 10¾″ Dinner Plate—Cobalt;

Page 35. Prego™ 20-Oz. Soup Bowl—Black

Page 36. VISIONS® 5-Quart Non-Stick Dutch Oven

Page 37. CORNING WARE® FRENCH WHITE® 2½-Quart Casserole with Serving Cradle; Prego™ Dinnerware—Black and White; CROWN CORNING® 7-Oz. Flute Champagnes; CROWN CORNING® Giverny™ Cake Serving Set; Elements™ THERMIQUE®—White

Page 38. Cranberry™ VISIONS® 2½-Quart Non-Stick Saucepan

Page 39. CORELLE® Impressions™ 15 Oz. Soup Bowl—Windward White™
Napkin: W. C. Imports

Page 40. Sculptured™ CORELLE® 18-Oz. Soup Bowl—Orchard Rose™
Napkins: James Crow & Co.

Page 42. Revere-Pro Line™ 6-Quart Dutch Oven

Page 44. Revere-Pro Line™ 10″ Saute Pan; CORELLE® NATURAL IMAGES® 10¼″ Dinner Plate—Hibiscus™

Page 47. Sculptured™ CORELLE® 12¼″ Serving Platter—Enhancements™

Page 48. Sculptured™ PYREX® 8″ Square Dish

Page 49. CORNING WARE® FRENCH WHITE® 1½-Quart Casserole
Tile: Nemo Tile; Napkin: W. C. Imports; Napkin ring: James Crow & Co.

For information on purchasing Corning Vitro products, please call the Corning/Revere Consumer Information Center at 800-999-3436.